Rising from the Ashes

My life as a killer, a convict who survived over 37 years in 17 prisons, and a man who beat the odds

By Gerald T. Balone

No Frills
<<<>>>
Buffalo

Copyright © 2012 Gerald T. Balone

All rights reserved. No part of this publication may be reproduced, stored in a retrieval system, or transmitted, in any form or by any means, electronic, mechanical, photocopying, recording, or otherwise, without the written prior permission of the author.

Printed in the United States of America

Balone, Gerald T.

Rising from the Ashes/ Balone 1st Edition

ISBN: 978-0615661711

1. Ashes – True Crime – Inspirational.   2. Philosophy – New Author – No Frills – Nonfiction.

No Frills Buffalo Press
119 Dorchester Road
Buffalo, New York 14213
For more information visit Nofrillsbuffalo.com

Rising from the Ashes

The picture on the cover was taken of Gerald Balone shortly after his arrest in 1973.

Some of us will endure things, so that others never have to. Be grateful for your past, no matter how ugly it is. Embrace it and share the truth of who you are with others. You might just save someone that is not as strong as you, the pain of enduring something horrible.

--Krista Ziedler

Chapter 1

It was a moment I had fantasized about for years – even decades. Yet when the gates of the Fishkill Correctional Facility closed behind me and I took my first deep breath as a free man in nearly 40 years, I felt anything but free.

I had spent more than half of my life behind bars and my identity had been reduced to that of prisoner No. 74-C-0264. Now I was suddenly in unfamiliar territory–*outside* the fences of the prison. Holding two potato sacks containing my worldly possessions with a modest check stuffed in the front pocket of my dress pants, my eyes darted to the left and then quickly back to the right.

I had heard all the stories before – prisoners released after serving their sentences, only to be met outside the gate by law enforcement ready to take them back into custody for some other crime.

No way is that going to be me, I thought to myself as I stood and waited, unsure of exactly what to do in those first moments of freedom. With no family or friends waiting to pick me up at the gate, I stood, nervously scuffing my shoes across the pavement, still waiting for the all-too-familiar sound of a barking correction officer (CO) ordering me back inside. But, it never came. Instead, I was shocked at the absolute silence.

After more than 37 years in prison, I was a free man. I had defied the odds and done what the guards and prisoners in 17 prisons all said was impossible. I had refused to listen when six different parole boards said I was unfit to be returned to society. Instead, I channeled my energy and my passion. Even though I had once been deemed one of the 64 most dangerous prisoners in the State of New York, I walked away from the hopelessness and misery that had enveloped so much of my life, and I knew I was never going back.

Thirty minutes after I was freed, a van pulled up to the gates of the medium-security prison and I climbed in. Freed of the handcuffs and leg irons that had been standard issue since I tried to escape from custody during a court appearance in the 1970s; I took a seat and stretched my legs. As the van pulled away, I looked back at the gray fence surrounding the prison, thick with barbed razor wire, and for the first time since they set me free, I allowed myself to smile. *I made it*, I thought to myself, *I made it*.

As was customary for all newly released convicts, the Department of Correctional Services (DOCS) van made a stop at a nearby bank so that each of us – there were two others besides me –could cash our prison-issued checks. As I stepped from the van and approached the front door of the bank, it was a surreal moment. Three of us walked into that bank, and instinctively, I wanted to let everyone know we weren't there to rob the place; we just wanted to cash our checks.

Considering the fact that I had lived under nearly 24-hour-a-day surveillance since I was convicted of brutally murdering three people during a home invasion in Buffalo, New York in 1973, I was accustomed to being watched with a suspicious eye. Whether it was the jury who convicted me, the judge who called my crime the most brutal he had ever seen, or the thousands and thousands of prisoners and correctional officers I had been locked in with over the last 30 plus years, I had learned to trust no one and I knew no one trusted me. Why should they? Anyone who had heard my story knew I was a two-bit hoodlum long before I broke into the small white house in a working-class Polish neighborhood and helped end the lives of three innocent people.

By the time I became a killer at the age of 20, I had already served more than three years in prison for armed robbery and had been arrested so many times, I lost count. I was a bad guy and everybody knew it, including me.

But the customers in the bank that day had no idea who I was. Gone was the prison-issued shirt with my prisoner number emblazoned across the breast pocket. To them, I was just another customer, here to do my business. It was my first act as a free man, and the simple act of cashing a check became symbolic of the struggles I would face in the weeks, months, and years ahead as I began the process of reintegrating myself into a city that had left me for dead almost four decades earlier.

Back in the van, they took us to a bus station with strict orders – for me, it was simple. I had a ticket in my pocket that would get me back to Buffalo, New York. I was to check in with my parole officer when I got to Cephas House, a halfway house for ex-convicts located in Buffalo's South Side. It was a journey that would take me north to the state capital of Albany, then West on Interstate 90 through Syracuse and Rochester before returning home. With more than two-dozen conditions of parole hanging over my head, I was scared. Forget the fact that in prison I worked hard to earn the reputation as the guy you didn't cross. When the ticket agent told me that I would be transferring and taking four different buses to reach Buffalo, panic set in. You've got to be kidding me, I told her. My mind began to race. I had forgotten what it was like to ride a bus that didn't have an armed guard on board. How was I supposed to navigate three more bus stations? What if I missed a connecting bus? Would they send me back? I knew the answer to that question, of course they would. Many people expected me to be back in prison eventually, so why not get the inevitable over with.

But I had worked too hard to get to this point, and I wasn't going to let some crazy bus schedule cost me the freedom I had so desperately worked for.

I walked away from the ticket window and scanned the crowd. People hustling on and off busses, couples embracing as they reunited, one of them was returning from a trip to who-knew-where. The sights and sounds were overwhelming, but strangely, it was the smells that drew my attention the most. After decades of surviving on prison food, and rations from the commissary, my olfactory senses were working overtime as the smells of French fries, hot dogs and pizza wafted through the terminal from nearby concession stands and vendors.

The thing was, when I woke up that morning, I knew there was no way I wanted any of that prison food in me when I left. So I skipped breakfast and now, I was hungry for something to eat.

The fact was, aside from the bus ticket, which was purchased with a state-issued voucher, I hadn't purchased anything in decades. Even then, most of what I acquired, I stole. The idea of walking up to a stand and asking for a hot dog overwhelmed me with possibilities. What if I miss my bus? How much money do I have? How much does a hot dog even cost? What would I do if someone tried to steal my two potato bags of personal belongings? The simplest questions were overwhelming, and so, I simply shuffled past the vendors, watching my fellow travelers eating slices of piping hot pizza and foot-long hot dogs slathered in mustard and relish. I did my best to ignore the feeling in the pit of my empty stomach and as I boarded the next bus, I reminded myself of one thing: I was free.

****

As the bus slowly rumbled out of the station, en route to the thruway and the next leg of the journey, I scanned the seats, taking in the minutest details of every passenger in the half-empty bus.

I wanted to talk to somebody, anybody. I wanted to grab the person next to me and say, hey, you want to hear a story.

Instead, I was surrounded by mostly young people whose ears were plugged with headphones, some linked into iPods, others to laptops, and each lost in their own world, oblivious to the fact that some of them were sitting just inches away from a triple murderer and career criminal. {This was a world I had absolutely no understanding of.}

Having entered prison for the second time in 1973, I had never used a cell phone, never operated a personal computer, nor purchased or listened to a CD. In fact, I had been incarcerated so long, technology had come and gone and come again during my life in lockdown. The Walkman, for example, was a technological revolution when it came to market in 1979. By that time, I was already five years into what I expected to be a life sentence, and before I would taste freedom, the Walkman would become a dinosaur of technology, replaced by the Discman, then the iPod.

I had been behind bars during seven different presidential terms, multiple wars, and advances in health, science and technology that the rest of the world took for granted. Now, I was learning firsthand how difficult life was going to be as I attempted to reintegrate myself back into society. Despite being surrounded by passengers, I felt totally alone. I was reminded of scenes I had watched in the movie, "Shawshank Redemption," when Brooks, and then Red were released from prison. I was as isolated on that bus, speeding across Interstate 90, passing through the farmland of upstate New York, as I had been during any of my many trips to solitary while in prison.

As morning turned to afternoon, and I nervously navigated a second and then a third bus station, I realized one thing –I was returning to a world infinitely different than the one I threw away back in 1973. Gone were decades of regimented, controlled living. No longer would I be told when to wake, when to sleep, what to wear, eat and say. The rules, regulations, and oppressive control were gone, but the uncertainty, fear, and almost child-like view of the world that remained would be a constant reminder in the weeks and months to come that there was a reason so many of the prisoners I saw walk out the prison gates through the years always seemed to return, usually rather quickly.

If the outside world was unforgiving to drug dealers, thieves and arsonists, how would they react to a man who was convicted of one of the most brutal crimes not only in the history of Buffalo, but in all of New York State? As I boarded my final bus of the day, bound for Buffalo, I was one step closer to finding out. I was operating on pure adrenaline. I knew I was about to return home. Considering that I was sent to prison with the assumption I would die behind bars, it was a bittersweet moment that not only would I never forget, but one I would remind myself of during the low points over the coming years. When doors were slammed in my face, jobs were offered and then rescinded, and basic necessities like food, clothes and shelter became a struggle to maintain, I would take myself back to the day of my release and remember that no matter how difficult things got, the worst day living on the toughest streets of Buffalo beats the misery out of a single day locked in a cage.

I knew all too well that most people expected me to reoffend and return to prison. After all, when they looked at me, all anyone saw, all they had ever seen was a criminal. I talk about how I went to prison a murderer and became more vicious behind bars. There were no doubts in people's minds that I would soon return to the only life I ever knew. The life that had been my destiny since my mother abandoned me at the hospital so many years ago and where I had spent the first 15 months of my existence at the Father Baker Infant Home for Children in Lackawanna, New York. I had worn all of the labels for so many years: retard, thug, career criminal, misfit, gangbanger, hoodlum and murderer. These were my identifiers. Other kids my age may have had Boy Scout merit badges; some had high school letters for their sporting prowess. I had neither. I was arrested for the first time at the age of eight. I could steal, hustle and survive on the streets in the way the Boy Scout could administer emergency first aid or the Varsity quarterback could throw a perfect spiral and hit his receiver in stride. All three might have a gift, but in my case, that gift would turn out to be a curse that would shape the person I became, the person who thought nothing of sticking a gun in the back of a woman as she exited the bank and robbing her. If you owed me money and I tracked you down, I would hurt you with the indifference of a man who saw life in terms of what the world owed me and all bets were off and it was a kill or be killed. It was the life I chose to live.

Chapter 2

To those who were busy buying tickets, saying their goodbyes or waiting for the arrival of their loved ones on the next bus, the bald man with the shaved head descending the steps of the bus dressed in black slacks and a button down shirt wouldn't have warranted a second glance. Upon closer inspection, an astute observer might have noticed that in lieu of luggage, or even a cheap duffel bag, I carried my possessions in two burlap potato sacks, courtesy of the kitchen at the Fishkill Correctional Facility. They certainly didn't match my attire, but then again, no one seemed to notice.

Following the strict conditions of my parole, I darted straight for the nearest payphone. I had been instructed to call Cephas House, the halfway house I would call home for the next three months. They were expecting me and a van would be dispatched to pick me up at the bus station.

There was only one problem. I'm standing there at the phone, putting in money, trying to call the number, and it isn't working. I couldn't figure out how to work a pay phone. These were different from the ones I knew before I went to prison. So I flagged down a passing traveler and gave the scrap of paper with the Cephas phone number scrawled on it, along with a pile of change into his hand. Can you help me make this call? I asked him.

Thirty minutes later, I was greeted by the first friendly faces I had seen all day. Three men came to chaperone me back to the halfway house: Mel, John and Roger. For me, they were a welcome sight.

It was crazy. They came running over to me and Mel, one of the guys in the group (and someone who has been in prison with me for 28 years), was screaming and yelling, and before you know it there were a number of police officers surrounding us and asking us what all of the noise is about. Among the more than two-dozen conditions of my lifetime parole, I couldn't have any contact with the police.

The officer came over and my friend told him, 'He just got out of prison after 37 years.' The cop told us we had to keep it down and I was like, man, I've been out one day and you're already getting me in trouble!

As the four of us, all ex convicts, climbed into the car outside the downtown bus station, my mind was racing. The Greyhound station is situated at the edge of the downtown business district, near the sprawling public library and the main campus of Erie Community College. But it is also less than two miles from 18 Olga Place, the scene of the murders.

If you exit the bus station and head East on Clinton Street, the separation between the haves and the have not's quickly becomes evident. Look in your rearview mirror and you see the downtown office buildings filled with lawyers, banking headquarters and county government. Look ahead and you see the blight and despair that is known as East Buffalo. Once a bustling part of the city that was home to Polish immigrants, when the city began to lose its industry the East Side was particularly hard hit. Today, the population is predominantly African-American; the modest clapboard homes that were once the source of pride for the families that lived there are now boarded up and abandoned by the thousands. Turn on the evening news and if there has been a shooting, too often it occurs on the tough streets of the East Side: Clinton, Bailey, Fillmore, Michigan, Kensington, William, Jefferson, Broadway, the streets are known for their gangs, drug activity, prostitution and street violence.

In 1973, the East Side was home to a gang that called themselves The Savage Ones. Made up of kids from broken homes, most with drug addictions, a penchant for violence and an aversion to work, members of the Savage Ones saw crime as their careers. I know because I was one of The Savage Ones and I was proud of it. As with all gangs, we had rules that we followed and if anyone disrespected us in any way, we had an obligation to retaliate - usually through some form of violence.

When I was 20, still just a kid really, a fellow Savage One, Tommy, and I decided to rob a house. It was how we lived. We didn't work, we stole. In this case I had gotten a tip from a guy who owed us money. The couple that lived there would be in Florida. Inside there was a valuable stamp and coin collection, ours for the taking. Bust a window, get in, get out and fence the merchandise. Easy work. Today, if you wind your way through the streets and make your way to the narrow passage known as Olga Way, you'll find an empty lot squeezed in between the run-down homes. Today it is a sandlot, but in the spring of 1973, 18 Olga Place became the site of one of the most infamous crimes the City of Buffalo had ever known.

****

"Are you hungry?"

Definitely, I told them, having not eaten a bite of food in more than 24 hours. I'm starving.

Though most prisoners might spend days, weeks, even years fantasizing about what their first meal would be as a free man would, I was different. In my final months in Fishkill, I spent my days running. I had become somewhat of a fitness nut in prison –partially as a product of survival and partially because it helped me clear my mind. Besides lifting weights and doing all sorts of calisthenics, I would run laps around the gravel track in the prison yard. While I ran, I would think. Despite entering prison barely able to read, after earning multiple degrees, I was a voracious reader predominantly of books dealing with psychology, self-help and business. Determined not to be one of the statistics, the men who use the front gate of the prison as a revolving door, I spent my days plotting and planning for a successful life on the outside. I had subsided largely on tuna fish, peanut butter, cereal, and packages of turkey purchased from the prison commissary (the latter which I was forced to store in my toilet to keep cold), food was not at the forefront of my mind. I was extremely proud of the fact that I did not smoke, drink alcohol, or coffee, or take any type of drug. I never added sugar, butter or seasoning to any of the food I ate in prison. I would eat whatever was placed in front of me. I never went to an honor block and never decorated my cell or cube like many of the men in prison had a habit of doing. I never allowed myself to become institutionalized and I deliberately lived in the worst blocks in all of the prisons I was at.

As we headed out of the city, we cruised along South Park Avenue and headed toward Lackawanna. Though it would later become internationally known as the home of the "Lackawanna Six," - the terrorists charged in the wake of Sept. 11, - Lackawanna is a small, working-class suburb of Buffalo. Once home to the workers of nearby Bethlehem Steel, today, with the bustling steel mill long gone, Lackawanna is another in the long stretch of impoverished suburbs on the outskirts of one of the poorest cities in America. At one time, it was also the place I called home.

The Wayside Restaurant is situated in South Buffalo and is your typical greasy spoon diner. The coffee is hot, portions are plentiful, and the booths are filled with "regulars."

As we entered the front door, the aroma of hot food hit my nostrils. Nearly lightheaded from hunger, and the emotion of the day, we made our way to a booth in the corner: I was prepared to devour my first meal in decades that didn't consist of low-grade government food. There was real silverware on the table. I had been eating with plastic fork/spoon (sporks) for most of my incarceration so it felt strange to see utensils laying in front of me that earlier that morning would have been considered weapons and could have landed me in solitary for months or longer.

Moments later a pretty young waitress appeared at the table. It had been a long time since I had interacted with a beautiful woman. Sure, there were prison visits, but most of the women that visited prisons certainly didn't look anything like the women I had seen at the bus station, or at the bank, and certainly not like the waitress.

"What can I get you gentlemen?" she asked, her voice syrupy with the undertone of a woman working for tips and serving a table of four men.

Mel piped up. "Get my friend here anything he wants," he said. "We're celebrating."

"Sounds good, what's the occasion?" she asked. He had no problem putting all my business out on the street.

"He just got out of prison after 37 years!"

The waitress looked pale. She paused, and seemed unsure of what to say, though not for the reason you might suspect. Finally, she gathered herself.

"Is your name Jerry?" she asked, locking eyes with me. Assuming my buddies were playing a goof on me, maybe setting me up since they had picked the Wayside, I smiled at the pretty young girl and decided to play along.

"Yeah, I'm Jerry, how did you know that?" I asked her, smiling.

"Because ... you're my uncle."

The words hung in the air for a moment. An occurrence that might have seemed like a million-to-one long shot to most people – a random coincidence, was anything but that to me. In the latter years of my incarceration I had come to develop a strong faith in God. Unlike the many "prison converts" who come to God as a means of impressing a parole board, gaining favor with a certain group on the inside or having an excuse to get out of their cell for religious services, my rebirth was different. I owed my religious awakening, and maybe my life, to a group of cloistered Dominican nuns from Elmira and Buffalo. The sisters had read about my crime and reached out to me, writing me letters in prison. Though it took the nuns years to break through the walls I had built to isolate myself from the outside world, they did break through; and this chance meeting, was in my mind, anything but "chance". It was an affirmation of what I knew to be true. God was watching over me and here I was, having woken up behind bars, sitting down to my first meal as a free man with no job, no money, wearing a triple murder conviction like a hair style, yet God extended a branch to me.

Five years later I struggle to recall what I ate for my first meal but I proudly show off the photo taken that night at the Wayside with my niece to everyone who comes to my house.

Two years later, I would end up doing the reading at church on the day of her wedding. I have come to love her two sons as if they were my own.

As we left the restaurant and climbed into the van for the short ride over to the halfway house that I would call home for the next three months, I allowed myself to take a deep breath and relax for the first time since the gates of Fishkill Correctional Facility had closed behind me that morning. I had worked too hard to get to this point, fought on through six failed parole hearings, and stayed alive for 37 years in some of the toughest prisons in the country. No matter what happened tomorrow, I was ready to take on life on the outside and insure I never became another entry in the long list of convicts who leave prison, only to return, usually within a few short months. *Not me*, I thought as we cruised along South Park Avenue, past the cheese factory, through the blue-collar neighborhoods and the retail stores that those out walking the streets took for granted. *Not ever.*

Chapter 3

It was a typical August day in Buffalo when I woke to begin my first day as a free man. The previous night I had arrived at Cephas House, a prison reintegration home in the city, to a welcome party. I was also given a bedroom, but after decades spent sleeping on little more than a steel slab with a thin mattress covering it, I soon found myself on the floor, unable to enjoy the thick soft mattress in my new home. I would later tell people this was a theme of life outside of prison. I may have been free, but after spending virtually my entire adult life in the system, there were parts of it I would never leave behind.

Come to my house today and you'll see my cupboards filled with three things. Tuna fish, peanut butter and cereal. They were the staple foods of my prison life, and like the bed, change would only come gradually. For some things, it wouldn't come at all.

My second day of freedom started out with me going to the Dominican Monastery on Doat Street to attend mass and watch a nun happily take her final vows to go behind the wall to spend the rest of her days living in a cell without watching television, reading a newspaper, listening to a radio, and dozens of other restrictions. As you can imagine, the parallel with my release and her loss of freedom was significant. It was almost as if she were taking my place behind prison walls… It was a beautiful ceremony and my admiration for the nuns became even stronger because she, along with the other sisters at the Monastery, will spend the rest of their lives praying for sinners like me…

After I left there, I was taken down to sign up for public assistance – food stamps, Medicare and other social service benefits. Though I lacked any formal education when I entered the prison system in the 70s, I soon found I could make a living selling everything from drugs, to cigarettes, to mice I smuggled in from the metal shops and coal gang. I later ran a successful gambling enterprise behind bars and did well from my illegal black-market efforts. Though it may sound strange to those unfamiliar with the way a prison works, if one looks at prison in the way we view society, I lived an upper middle class existence for much of my incarceration. I had money, access to clothes, good food, cigarettes, cash, most anything could be had – for a price. Behind bars I could collect a couple of cartons of smokes from a gambling wager, then broker a deal with a prisoner who works in the kitchen to smuggle out a few fresh chickens. I never cooked: I didn't have to. Two chickens were handed off to a prisoner with a hotplate, another prisoner with a bag of rice and some beans stopped by, and before you knew it, we were dining on a gourmet meal that a free man might pay $25 for at some upscale restaurant.

Now, on the outside, just blocks from such restaurants, I found myself signing up for food stamps. Though I knew it wasn't going to be easy when I got out, it was a humbling moment for me – I truly believed my two Masters degrees and countless commendations earned while in prison were going to mean something on the outside. As I filled out the paperwork to get my benefits card, I realized for the first time that my accomplishments and accolades meant nothing to the vast majority of people I would encounter. To them, I was just another felon – someone to fear, someone to cross the street if you saw walking toward you, someone to dismiss and assume would be returned to his rightful place in prison sooner rather than later. I was determined to prove them all wrong.

My first weeks at Cephas were hard. The rules of the program were strict –residents were required to commit to a minimum stay of three months. For me, having spent years visualizing my eventual freedom, I knew this was a small step in the long journey I was on. Before I left prison, I was sent a list of the rules I would have to follow at Cephas and even though I felt some of them made no sense at all (just like most of the rules in prison), I knew that I would abide by all of them.

I was free technically, but not really. According to Brother Mike, who ran the program at Cephas, there is a reason behind the 90-day commitment. While recidivism rates may be incredibly high for felons leaving prison, 75 percent of residents who complete the program at Cephas, never return to prison.

I didn't care for the rules –including a strict curfew - despite being a man who had never had a bank account, driven a car, registered to vote, filled out a job application, owned a credit card, paid a bill, or rented an apartment, the transition was going to be challenging. I knew that, and so I spent my first few weeks in the program learning in the way a baby learns to walk. There was plenty of encouragement from the staff and fellow ex-convicts, mixed with those awkward first steps; plenty of trips and falls, and eventually, the ability to wobbly navigate my way unaccompanied.

I truly believe that anyone who has been incarcerated for a significant amount of years should go to a halfway house upon his or her release. People in the free world may have an idea of what their loved one experienced while on the inside, and all of the emotions he's dealing with once released. But people in halfway houses know exactly what the transition is like and are there to answer questions and slowly reintegrate the person back into society. If I would have had to go to work within a few days of my release, there's no way I could have done so because everything was so different from when I first went to prison.

****

My freedom wasn't some random act –the impulse of a liberal parole board or the result of a pardon from some outgoing politician. My release from prison came as the young man who first entered prison barely able to read or write - evolved and matured; and (over decades) learned to navigate the legal system, to get along - and was finally, carefully able to craft my eventual release. White it was the parole board that signed off on my release, I worked for it: toiling for years on end, writing letters, taking classes, reading every book I could and I studied how the process went for every prisoner who appeared before the board, to analyzing what they did right if they earned parole and what they did wrong if they were given another two years.

With my meticulous preparations, I came to a master plan for life as a free man. In the years preceding my release from Fishkill, I spent hours walking the gravel track of the prison yard with dual purposes. First, I worked religiously to keep my body in peak physical condition, as both a means of survival and in preparation for my next life. Equally important though, would be the mental workout I put in on the track.

I planned my entire life. Everything I'm doing right now, I knew I'd be doing because I thought about it every day. I visualized it, and I knew -if they let me out - I was going to be ready to make everything happen. No way was I ever coming back.

Though I had no intentions of returning to prison, surviving on the outside was going to be a challenge. I returned to Buffalo with no money, no job, no friends, no prospects and I carried my worldly possessions in those two old potato sacks. I would be staying at a halfway house for the 90-day minimum I had committed to. The way I saw it, I had 90 days to put my plan in motion. After spending most of my adult life under constant watch, I had no intention of living in a prison outside of prison.

Chapter 4

One hundred days after I walked away from Fishkill Correctional Facility, I packed my modest possessions and left Cephas House. I found a house in Buffalo, signed a lease, gave a deposit and had a place that was my own. I was 56 years old.

Western New York is a sprawling landmass surrounding the City of Buffalo with a population in excess of one million people. With large pockets known as blue-collar working communities, housing is shockingly affordable to those who come from other parts of the country. I had options. To the north, I could have settled into Niagara Falls, which despite its famous waterfalls is a tough city where a man of my dubious past stood as good a chance of blending in as anywhere. I could have opted to go south, finding an apartment in Lackawanna,

Blasdell, or any of the smaller, rural communities that are collectively referred to by locals as The Southtowns.

In 2007, I could have found a clean, modest apartment in any of these areas for $400 or less, a price I could manage between finding odd jobs and social service benefits.

Despite the options that lay before me, I made a decision that seemed alternately shocking, offensive, or perfectly logical, depending on whom you asked. I rented a home on Bristol Street in the heart of Buffalo's tough East Side. At first glance, it seemed like a good place for a murderer to call home. After all, I was far from the only killer to call East Buffalo home.

But Bristol Street was home in more ways than one. Bristol intersects with Clare Street, and in the spring of 1973 I was living in a run-down clapboard home at 109 Clare Street when I hatched the plan to break-into a home and rob its owners of their coin and stamp collection.

I was returning to the old neighborhood and if I thought the people of East Buffalo had forgotten what happened more than

30 years earlier, I was wrong. Other than my landlord, it soon became evident that no one wanted a notorious triple-murderer living among them. If that weren't enough, I had taken up residence just a quarter mile from 18 Olga Place, the scene of the murders. I now hung my hat two blocks, less than the length of four football fields, from the place where I helped brutally murder three innocent people.

In a city of more than 52 square miles, with thousands of homes and apartments for rent, I did what so many others before me had done – I returned to the last place I had called home.

****

There were two distinct advantages to living on the East Side of Buffalo that drew me to the house on Bristol Street. First, those who could afford to were fleeing the area, giving way to the drug lords and gangbangers who had taken over what was once an area filled with hard working Polish immigrants. I was in the unique position of fearing no one. I had survived 37 years in some of the most God-awful hellholes in America surrounded by some of the most anti-social, violent people who ever lived. I walked away without so much as a single scar on my body. As others around me were regularly beaten, raped, and even killed inside prison, I managed to serve my time and walk away physically unscathed. I sure wasn't afraid of the East Side thugs roaming the streets. The first advantage led directly to the second. As one might imagine, people weren't exactly knocking down the doors to move into homes on the East Side, so I was able to rent an entire house, complete with a large bedroom, eat-in kitchen, living room, dining room, laundry room, and office, for $350 per month.

I had spent so many years living in a cage, in a cell or cube not any bigger than my new bathroom, that I wanted a big place, where I was alone. I didn't want people living above me, or below me, I wanted to be alone.

There was also the fact that I was on lifetime parole with a laundry list of restrictions. Sharing a building with neighbors also had the potential to invite trouble into my life, and that wasn't a risk I was willing to take.

I moved into 349 Bristol Street on December 1, 2007 with little more than I carried with me from prison. With no bed, I slept on the floor. I had no kitchen table, but then again, I didn't plan to do much cooking or entertaining. No couch, no television, not much of anything. I bought myself a little hot pot like the one I had in prison. I used that to boil water for my tea. I had my freedom and I had quiet, two things that had eluded me for most of my life.

If I was worried about people bothering me in my new place, I didn't need to. People avoided me. Once word spread of my arrival – and in a place like East Buffalo, word travels fast – people began to talk. If I left my house to take a walk, neighbors would gather up their children from the front yard and quickly go inside. People walking to their cars would cast their eyes to the ground and avoid any conversation. Among themselves, the whispers began. People who didn't know the story were quickly filled in, taking liberty with the facts behind my story. People wondered out loud how long it would be before police cars came screeching to a halt in front of the red house at the end of the street and I was dragged out the side door in handcuffs, for

God-only-knows what heinous crime. Fortunately, time would prove them all wrong.

****

Though the police never broke down the door and hauled me back to prison, they were watching me. I may have walked away from prison, but my strict conditions of parole at times made me feel like a prisoner within my new home. There was a strict curfew. I was not permitted to leave my house before 7 a.m., and had to be inside by 9 p.m. There were, of course, no drugs or alcohol, no fraternizing with any convicted felons – the people who I had called family for my entire life. The list went on and on, and all of it was enforced by parole officers conducting random checks of my home.

Upon entering, at any time of the day or night and without notice, I would be told to sit in a chair in the middle of my kitchen while my parole officer, sometimes in the company of other parole officers went through every drawer, cabinet and box in the entire house. They could examine my computer, listen to my messages on the answering machine and inspect the contents of the refrigerator. Nothing was private and the smallest slip-up would have earned me a one-way ticket back to prison. I was, and still am, operating without a net. My freedom comes with so many strings attached I feel like a marionette doll – but at least one that is free.

I'm probably the most law-abiding citizen out here. I never go over the speed limit, I don't litter, I don't so much as jaywalk, because I am never going back to prison and I know there are people just waiting for me to slip up so they can send me back.

Despite all of the restrictions placed upon me and the fact that I was living in a virtual fishbowl among my suspicious neighbors, I was still a free man, and now that I had left the confines of Cephas House behind me, I was ready to put my plan in motion. I knew what I wanted and my years of planning, strategizing and visualizing were about to pay off ... or so I thought.

Chapter 5

You don't survive nearly four decades in prison without mastering a few critical skills. First and foremost, you must be able to size up and read any person on a moment's notice. One look at them and you need to be able to decipher if they are a junkie you could sell to, a gambler you could loan to, a booty bandit who needed to know your ass was off-limits if he expected to live, a person with mental problems that needed to be avoided, a killer, or a stand-up guy you might be able to trust. Even before I had earned my bachelor's degree in psychology, I had learned how to size people up. It's how I survived 17 prisons. I tell people, I went to prison a killer and I became more of a criminal in there than I was out here in the free world. Just like on the outside, being able to size up your opponent and stay two steps ahead of them is critical to your survival and success.

When I left Fishkill and climbed aboard that bus, I knew things were going to be tough. I had heard the stories of life on the outside for an ex-convict. I knew how many guys I had seen walk out the gates of every prison I had ever been in, all with the same cocky proclamation that they would never be back, only, to see them processed back in, two, three, six months later.

I had read all of the statistics, the articles, and the books. I knew the odds were stacked against me, and yet, as hardened as I was, a vicious killer who had spent a lifetime robbing, beating and murdering people as a means to an end, I returned to the free world a bit naive.

I really thought it was going to be different for me. I had earned two master's degrees along with many other academic and therapeutic credentials. I had read all of the books and had asked thousands of questions of those who had been free and returned to prison. I had taken all of the programs and I thought there would be opportunities for me on the outside that these other guys didn't have.

I was wrong.

My degrees:

Associate of Science from Ulster County Community College

Bachelor's with a dual major in Sociology and Psychology from SUNY New Paltz

Master's in Urban Ministry from New York Theological Seminary

Master's in Healthcare Administration & Wellness Promotion from California College for Health Sciences

One semester with Mercy College - received 18 credits

Three Department of Labor certifications with well over 5000 hours in each:

- Pre-release Counseling Aide
- Drug and Alcohol Counseling Aide
- HIV/AIDS Counseling/Prevention Aide

Over those years "inside", I taught college courses and attended dozens of therapeutic programs and went on to become a facilitator and coordinator in many of them. I left prison with a portfolio full of certificates and awards and was sure that people would be knocking down my doors to offer employment.

My credentials might have helped win over a parole board, but the general public didn't care how rehabilitated or educated I was. Prospective employers looked past the education, looked past my warm and engaging personality and instead saw one thing on my resume: triple murderer. Sure, it wasn't literally on there, but it came up on every single background check and it was the final nail in the coffin of every potential job opportunity.

Even if a prospective employer didn't conduct a background check (and they all did) I had made myself a promise when I walked out of prison: I was never going to lie about who I was and what I did. I wasn't going to hide from my past and if people were going to be part of my life, I wanted them to know who I was.

It was a noble concept and one that would eventually reap benefits in other areas of my life, but for a man who now had the responsibility of paying rent, utilities, and living expenses for the first time, it made things challenging.

My life plan had included landing a job that would allow me to put my education to use, and then begin to build a business as an author and motivational speaker. I had done what everyone had deemed impossible. Few people commit a triple homicide and ever see the light of day again. I had been sentenced to 50 years to life, meaning I wasn't even eligible for parole until I was 70-years-old. Yet at the age of 56, I was a free man. I had served time in Attica in the 1970s as well as 16 other prisons and yet I had walked away physically and mentally intact. No HIV, no hepatitis, and no alcohol or drug addiction as is so common among my former fellow prisoners. I left prison educated, healthy and hungry to build the life I saw as my destiny. I saw my story as the ultimate inspirational tale, a story so good, that if there wasn't the proof it was real, would seem like something out of a make-up Hollywood movie.

During those long hours in lockup, I had developed a detailed business plan. I would use the money I planned to save from working to start my business. In addition to writing books aimed at prisoners and their families – books that would impart my wisdom of not only how to survive prison, but how to *legally* escape (i.e.: earn parole) I saw myself traveling the country speaking to large groups with an inspirational message built around "If I could succeed, anybody can."

Instead, six months after being released from prison, I was subsiding on food stamps, food banks, soup kitchens and the generosity of neighbors and the people I had begun to meet in the spiritual community.

No one wanted to hire me, so I began to volunteer at the food pantry, soup kitchen, and many other places. I volunteered at churches, and everywhere I went, I introduced myself to everyone, told them who I was and asked them if they had any work.

Slowly, the approach began to pay off. I started to land the occasional job cleaning out the gutters of a sympathetic parishioner, cleaning out a basement, raking leaves, shoveling snow, moving furniture, and cleaning houses. Some of my neighbors have become my best friends and there were many times when they invited me into their homes for dinner.

I never thought with two master's degrees coming out, that I would be scrubbing people's toilets. It was a tough pill to swallow. I was once one of the most feared and powerful prisoners in the State of New York, now reduced to this. Whether it was during my early years when I was a drug dealer, or later when I moved on to run a gambling enterprise and commanding the respect of fellow prisoners, I had been somebody. Even as I reformed my ways and sought out education and self-help, the other prisoners admired me. It may sound odd to those who have never served time, but the prison subculture is a strange beast, and within the underworld of the penal system, I was a good guy.

Walking away from that life with such high expectations of success, only to find myself on my knees scrubbing someone's floor was more than a humbling experience, it was nearly crippling.

Add to that the fact that I had offers on the outside to utilize my considerable black market talents to earn real money, and it would have been easy to return to the only life I had ever known, almost certainly punching my ticket back to prison. During my years locked up, I had befriended everyone from low-level street dealers to mob bosses. Living in a system where bartering and favors are the methods of survival, I had earned my share of good will among some of the most violent, wild people in the State of New York. My reputation as a stand-up guy willing to do whatever was necessary to protect myself inside had earned me respect among my fellow prisoners. In 37 years inside I had never ratted out a single time. There were plenty of chances. Guards would ply me with offers of better food and more privileges to sell out a fellow prisoner. There were also threats –promises of a lengthy stay in solitary if I didn't speak. I took the isolation every time, refusing to violate the prison code and for that, the dealers, loan sharks and mob bosses were grateful. Before I even hit the street I was fielding offers. There were calls to make and names to drop that would guarantee me a comfortable income on the outside. Cash in a few favors and I could be driving a new car, dressing in the best clothes and living the life I had been dreaming about for so many years.

The work – well that would be easy. I had spent a lifetime hustling. I grew up as a thief, a con man, and a person with no remorse, willing to do whatever it took to survive. The way I saw things in that time "before prison," the world had messed me over and it was payback time. If you were walking out of the bank with an envelope full of cash, forget that you had worked all week to earn that money. In my eyes you were a lucky, spoiled person who got all the breaks I never did. You could never fathom my life and all of the abuse, pain and suffering I had endured. I could follow you around the corner, stick a gun into your back and rob you without a second thought. You need that money for groceries. Too bad. You've got kids at home? Not my problem. I was a kid who had grown up in a home where I was hated by my mother and often ran away, choosing to sleep in junkyards and dog houses rather than my own home so family had very little meaning to me. The most lasting thing my mother had ever given me was a gnarled patch of flesh on my right hand when she decided to punish me by holding my hand down on the hot stove. The scars are still visible today. I survived nearly four decades in prison and the only scars on my body were inflicted by the woman who gave birth to me and to all of the people who were entrusted to take care of me as a child. So in my mind back then, forget you and your family. I was a street survivalist and I was a master of my craft.

The story was the same for my first two decades behind bars. I didn't go looking for trouble, but inside the walls of a prison, trouble has a way of finding you. In the 1970s when I was a drug dealer at Attica, there would always be the junkie who didn't pay up when it was commissary time.

If I let him off, people would know I was soft. But if I give him a beating in the yard I'm going to solitary and then I can't collect the rest of the money that people owe me.

Notice there is no emotion in these words. This isn't about right and wrong in the traditional sense. There is no hesitation at the thought of brutally beating a man. No qualms about breaking someone's jaw or worse. The hesitation is in the beating potentially costing me money or freedom. You don't survive in prison for as long as I did without being wired a bit different than the rest of the world. Unfortunately, for those who wronged me, that meant they would suffer.

So in what was prison justice, I would wait. And wait. Eventually, the junkie would slip up. He might stray into a part of the prison where the guards couldn't see. The stairwells were a great place to settle the score. Like an animal in the wild, I would stalk my prey, waiting for the perfect moment to strike. Moments later I would emerge from the concrete stairwell flecked in blood. I would quickly retreat to my cell and clean myself up. For the unfortunate person who had decided to cross me, it wouldn't be so easy. He lay crumpled against the stairs; his moans were eventually heard by the CO's who would rush in to find him bloody and broken. The word gets out. Do it a few times and you tend to have a lot less difficulty collecting your money.

It really isn't any different than life on the outside.

If the boss comes through and fires a few people, the word gets out and the rest of the employees work harder because they don't want to be next.

Though I spent the last decade of my incarceration walking the straight path, working on my education, my rehabilitation and in becoming the man I am today, for me, the violence is like riding a bike. You may go decades without doing it, but if you have to, you can climb right back on and start pedaling.

But I knew if I was going to beat the odds and live out my remaining years as a free man, I could never go back to that lifestyle. The parole board believed I would do the right thing. Many of my fellow prisoners assumed they would see me again. It was just the way it went. You got out, couldn't make it in the free world and you eventually returned to the life where you felt comfortable. A life where if you were me, you garnered respect unlike anything you could hope for on the outside. In prison, I was both feared and respected. On the outside the fear was still there, but the respect would take years to earn, and in most cases, would never come.

Still, I had a plan and I was committed to seeing it through. So no matter how tough times got –and they got very tough –I never made the phone call. The drug money would have been easy, I could have earned a comfortable living stealing, working as an enforcer or booking. With a house located in the center of one of the most poverty stricken, drug-infested, hopeless parts of any American city, the customers would have flocked to me like shooting fish in a barrel.

But the idea of redemption wasn't just some empty words I offered up to a parole board. I meant it. I believed it. And I intended to live it.

That's not to say I don't walk the fine line between redemption and reoffender. Today, at 59-years-old and several years removed from prison, I am a passive character. But look deeply into my eyes, study my mannerisms, analyze my words and you'll see a man you would still be well advised not to cross. But I hadn't come this far to throw it all away. As I hauled trash, cleaned toilets and paid for my groceries with a government handout, I plotted my course. It may have proven to be tougher than I expected, but I had no intention of giving up. If anything, for every job interview that went nowhere, for every door slammed in my face, for every visit from my parole officer, my resolve hardened.

Having survived a childhood of torture and abuse the likes of which few people can imagine and an adult life spent almost entirely behind bars, it was going to take a lot more than this to break me.

I just kept telling myself, I would do whatever it took. If I had to give up my apartment and go to a shelter, that's what I would do. If I had to eat at the soup kitchen, I would do it. It didn't matter to me, because no matter what, it was better than going back to prison, and I believed in my heart that everything I had envisioned was going to happen for me, it was just going to take longer than I thought.

Chapter 6

There are two sides to the City of Buffalo. There is the side best known to outsiders – the city's proximity to the majestic wonder that is Niagara Falls; its claim to fame for the invention of the Buffalo Wing; and its reputation for having some wild winter weather. Ask any outsider to name three things about Buffalo and you'll likely hear wings, weather and "I drove through there once on the way to Niagara Falls." Historical buffs might even think of Buffalo as the sight of the assassination of the 25th President of the United States, William McKinley.

But there is another side to Buffalo, a side of urban despair, abject poverty and racial divide that has landed the once booming industrial city near the top of every list of the poorest cities in America.

It was that side of Buffalo that I returned to after my release and it was there, on the gritty streets of the East Side where I started out to put into motion my self-made plan for rehabilitation.

Though I had visions of speaking before a standing-room only crowd in auditoriums across America sharing my life story of rehabilitation and redemption, clad in a custom-tailored suit and exiting the stage to thunderous applause, reality, as it often is, was quite different.

I knew I had a message for troubled youth, and for those adults whose job it was to guide and protect them, but when you are a convicted triple-murderer, most people are less than enthusiastic about opening their doors to you.

When they did open their doors, they were in for a harsh reality starting with what became my standard opening remarks: On August 14, 2007 I was released from prison after serving over 37 and one half years for killing three people during a robbery. It wasn't exactly a textbook icebreaker.

Nonetheless, relying on my faith in God, and maybe more importantly, my faith in myself, I forged on. When traditional doors were repeatedly slammed in my face, both literally and figuratively, I turned to the people I suspected would be most open to hearing my message: The Church. Between my time spent at Cephas House and my time volunteering at the local soup kitchen and shelters, I had met my share of church folks. I shared my story with every one of them, offering to speak at their respective churches no matter where or when. Eventually, a few people took me up on the offer and finally, more than a year after I had walked away from prison, I began the next step of my reincarnation.

Though Jerry Balone, cold-blooded killer would always be there, I began the first steps to shove him out of the spotlight in favor of Jerry Balone, a man of God who sought forgiveness for a life gone astray and found redemption through his current words and deeds.

****

I have three basic rules when I speak before a group, be it three people in a church conference room or 300 people packing a sanctuary or auditorium. They are part of the business model I created during my final years in Fishkill and for the first time I was seeing the fruits of my mental labor begin to blossom.

Just like on the street, I never hold back anything when I tell my story. It doesn't matter if I am speaking to the order of friars at St. Bonaventure University or to a group of teens, every detail is the same –and it is graphic. I'm not going to water it down. Rule number two: answer every question. If I am going to stand in front of an audience packed with teenagers, often in an urban school setting and tell them the story of how I spent a lifetime as a career criminal, how I went on to brutally murder three innocent people and spent 37 years in prison, it comes with a price. There will always be the kid on a dare, or the class clown, or just a plain wiseass who wants his moment in the spotlight. It happens virtually every time, and when the brave youngster would slip his hand up and I acknowledge him, invariably he offers something along the lines of, "So, all those years in prison, did you ever drop the soap in the shower?"

I know it is all part of the territory – like the people on the street who will never forgive me for what I did and believe I should be dead; the soap jokes are part of the deal.

I look them right in the eye and say, "Do I look like I dropped the soap? If we both went to prison right now, it would be you that is going to end up somebody's girlfriend."

The last line will often elicit giggle from the students, but the looks on their faces tell another story as well –I am telling the cold hard truth, something many of them have never heard before. The impact of the message is clear, and in the early years of giving the talk, the emails and letters I received from students sharing their own stories filled with family secrets, pain and struggles reinforce that I am on the right track. There is a need in the community – and in the world, and I want to use my remaining years to fill that empty void I see in the faces, hear in the voices and read in the letters of so many students.

Chapter 7

It had been almost five years since I had last spent a night in prison. Five years since I had eaten the food or taken orders from the guards. Five years since I had been forced to strip naked and bend over and spread my ass cheeks apart so some guard could check to see what I might be hiding up there. I was free, and though I appreciated every breath of fresh air I took and every morning I woke in my own bed, life on the outside was every bit the struggle I had heard it would be.

In the fall of 2010, I was living in the $350 month house I rented on Buffalo's East Side. I was driving a late model Toyota, thanks to a government program called Cash for Clunkers and I was working part-time at Alcohol and Drug Dependency Services, an inpatient rehab center in Buffalo. I disliked many things about the job, but when you have a resume that includes a 40-year gap in your employment history and a background check that turns up three murders, you can't be too choosy. I was biding my time. The job was mostly working overnight, essentially supervising the clients to make sure they weren't sneaking out, smuggling in drugs, or disobeying any of the other rules. I was being asked to act like some of the guards who used to watch over me in prison and I didn't care for it but it paid the bills and it allowed me to have my days free to travel to schools and talk with students, but other than that, I hated many of the concepts that were taught to the clients at the agency.

In most rehabs, the clients are constantly told they have a lifetime disease and are powerless to overcome it and that relapse is part of their treatment. The recidivism rate at many of these places is even worse than it is for people returning to prison. It seems like many of the clients say and do all of the right things in order to play the system. Many are court mandated or on probation and parole. Many have outstanding criminal charges pending and they suspect that if they complete the program that the judge will give them a break.

I have two master's degrees and I was doing a job that required a high school education. But I knew better than to waste a single opportunity so I used the overnights to prepare. I purchased a laptop computer and continued to seek out speaking opportunities, publicity for my case (I desperately wanted to get out from under the oppressively restrictive rules of my parole), and business opportunities. It was also about this time that I began to embrace social media as a way to share my story and make more connections. *Use every opportunity to promote yourself and to meet new people.* But as the requests from schools to have me share my "shock story" increased social media also became a practical way to connect with my predominantly teen audience. Joining the ranks of Facebook, Twitter, BranchOut, LinkedIn, Pinterest, and others, I found a way to reach even more people with my message. While my strict parole kept me mostly confined to speaking in Western New York, suddenly I had a venue to literally speak to the world. At each event I would hand out business cards and encourage the students to "friend" me on the social networking site. Soon I had nearly 5,000 followers and was sharing inspirational messages, updates on speaking engagements and information on proposed laws and changes in the justice system. Social media did two things: First, it allowed me to reach a much broader audience with my message; but second, it reminded me of something I had long known. I wanted to – needed to – share my story not just with a few hundred students or parishioners at a time, but with a worldwide audience. Facebook was my first sense that my story could make a difference on a global scale.

****

The Regional office of the New York State Division of Parole (NYSDOP) is located on Main Street in downtown Buffalo, New York. The office is bordered by abandoned storefronts inhabited by people begging spare change and nursing bottles wrapped in brown paper bags purchased from the tiny Bodega next door. Yet in stark contrast, it also sits in the shadow of the Liberty Building, a Buffalo landmark office tower that is home to some of the most powerful law firms, financial firms and corporations in the state. On any given afternoon, businessmen suited up and on their way to their next power lunch share the sidewalk with the drug addicts, alcoholics, violent felons and other scofflaws who line up outside the parole office waiting for the doors to open.

The scene is a perfect snapshot of modern-day Buffalo: abject poverty, despair and hopelessness, blended with just enough success and possibility to keep the city from imploding.

As part of my litany of parole conditions, I have to report to the parole office regularly. When I first got out, it was weekly, then bi-weekly, then once a month and now it is four times a year. It's a rubber-stamp job, but miss a single appointment and I would face a return to prison, never to taste freedom again. Each visit I am required to stand in line and wait. The NYSDOP is badly overburdened and any true sense of rehabilitation is out of the question. Wait your turn. Pay your parole fee charges and eventually get to sit with your parole officer, maybe the one who knew your case, maybe not, and get pushed along out the door. Ask anyone who is on parole or has been on parole and they will tell you their biggest fear is going to see their parole officer and getting arrested and hauled off to jail on a parole violation. Even though I know I am always doing the right thing, I still live with this fear and after my seeing my parole officer; I always feel a great sense of relief.

As I exited the building after one such visit, I made my way down Main Street., my mind in overdrive as always. As I crossed over the train tracks and headed back to my car, I passed by a bench where a single discarded newspaper caught my eye. Always mindful of using the media to share my story of redemption and build my brand, I stopped and picked it up. Across the top of the masthead in blue script it read, *Buffalo Law Journal*. In a city dominated by *The Buffalo News*, owned by billionaire Warren Buffet, I had never heard of the newspaper. I wasn't alone. Not many people outside of the legal community had. Despite its existence for more than 80 years, the *Law Journal* was a niche publication with a small, albeit loyal, subscriber base. But I knew none of that. As I tucked the newspaper under my arm and continued on my way, I gave it very little thought. I would do the same thing I had done countless times before. I would call the editor, send an email, and pitch my story. Always the optimist, the way I figured it, it just took that one person –the right person—to hear my story and it would be the tipping point I had been waiting for to launch the next phase of my life. Eventually someone from the paper contacted me and arrangements were made for a reporter to write a story about the work that I was doing to keep young people out of the criminal justice system. Many articles had already been written about the work I was doing but somehow, I felt this was going to be different.

Chapter 8

The next day, I was scheduled to speak to a group of students at Harvest House in South Buffalo which is used as a retreat center for people from all over the world. Though Harvest House is located in a gritty, blue-collar part of the city, the students were coming from a private high school and the reporter said he wanted to come, said he was curious to see how I interacted with the students and more importantly, how they viewed a triple murderer standing in their midst. We had already spoken on the phone and he was familiar with my story. He had mentioned at the end of our interview that he was going to come by for more material for the article. Yet when he rounded the corner and I saw him approaching, I was surprised.

He eased into the room and quietly slipped into a corner. Though he was officially there to take photos to accompany the article, I knew he was there to analyze me, see if I had told the truth the day before in our interview and see if he was going to write the article. I was on display, and something told me this article could be a game-changer. But it didn't matter who was there. I gave my presentation the way I always did. If he liked it and wrote the article, great. If he thought I should have been executed and left the room, never to speak to me again, that was fine too.

I knew what he was thinking, the same way I knew what everyone I dealt with was thinking. Reading people is easy, especially when you have been doing it as long as I have and doing it as a means of survival. He wondered how graphic I would get with the private school boys. Would I talk about men raping other men in the showers? Would I talk about full body cavity searches, learning to use the bathroom in full view of other people and the extreme violence that is so pervasive inside the walls of prison?

I spent much of the interview the day before touting my ministry. But I knew what he thought. He saw me the same way everyone else did: killer first and anything else second. He wanted to know if the "ministry" was just a front. Another in the long line of cons that I used to survive countless foster homes, orphanages, detention centers, reform schools, and later survive 37 plus years in prison? Was it a scam to elicit sympathy? Money? Job offers? All of the above? They were questions that lots of people asked themselves and I could tell he wasn't any different. But once I stepped up in front of the group, I didn't even see him standing there. I was in the zone, and this was just another talk, one of hundreds since the shackles came off and I returned to the world a free man.

Chapter 9

As I spoke to the group, I told them the real deal –at least part of it. I told them what they needed to hear, but it doesn't take much to scare them straight. At least not for the ones who need to be scared. When I look into a crowd, I can tell the kids who are on the path I was on at their age. They give it away in their eyes; they give it away in their body language; they give it away in the conversation after I am done. Sometimes, they give it away in the questions they ask.

So when it comes to my life –to my crimes, I give them an overview. They know what you know to this point: I robbed a house with an accomplice; we thought the people were on vacation and when they were home and confronted us, we killed them. That is all true. But there is so much more to the story than that. I don't focus on it because it isn't what my story is about. My crime is merely a focal point; it is an event that happened to set everything else in motion. But I don't dwell on it when speaking publicly because I don't want to glorify what I did.

People ask me if I am sorry for what I did. Of course I am. I wish it had never happened. I wish we had never heard about some stupid coin and stamp collection. I wish they had gone on vacation. I wish a lot of things had gone differently in my life. But they didn't and like all of you, I have to live with the choices I have made. But I also don't use my crime. I don't want to profit on the deaths of three innocent people. I don't want to tarnish them or cause any extra pain for their families.

What I do want to do is use what happened *after* the murders as a way to teach kids about consequences and to show them that living some kind of thug life, or being a gangster is a dead end street.

But there are those of you reading this that want and need to know what happened. You want to know more. I suppose if I am asking you to listen to my path to redemption, that story isn't complete without knowing what happened on the night of April 23 into the morning of April 24, 1973.

I was a Savage One. What did that mean? Basically, we were a collection of hoodlums. We didn't work and most of us came from broken homes: we were largely an uneducated group of misfits who embraced the criminal lifestyle. When we needed something, we stole it. We stole from stores, we stole from people, and we stole from homes. It was how we survived and I never thought anything of it at that time.

Cash was the best. If I could catch you coming out of the bank and do a quick stick-up, that was gold. Back then, there were no ATM's or debit cards. People went to the bank on payday and walked out with an envelope full of cash. I could watch you, follow you as you left the bank, and wait for you to turn the corner. I'd slide in behind you, stick a gun in your back and the envelope was mine. Nobody is willing to fight back for the money when they feel the gun in their ribs. It was a relatively easy way to make a living, as least it was until I got pinched for one of these stick-ups. It was in the early 1970s and I got hit with three and a half years and spent time in Elmira, Coxsackie, and Comstock. I was 17-years-old.

Prison in the 1970s wasn't what it is like today. The idea of prisoners' rights didn't exist. Prisons were violent, hate-filled places where people were assaulted and killed over the littlest things. I might have been a teenager, but I went in there with as much bravado as anyone. I knew that was my only chance to survive. Besides, I may have been 17 biologically, but my life forced me to grow up fast and I had a lifetime of hurt and pain to channel as I served my time.

I should have gotten out in 18 months but I had an inability to follow rules and regulations. I was always challenging authority and going to solitary never bothered me. I was used to being punished and considered it a challenge to accept and get through any restrictions imposed on me by prison authorities. In solitary, I would do thousands of push-up, sit-ups and other exercises all day long and dream of the day of my release so I could go out and commit new crimes that would allow me to live happily ever after. I had taken no educational or therapeutic programs and I had no intention of leading a law-abiding life. I definitely left prison in 1973 much worse than when I entered the system three years earlier. I was full of hate and bitterness and ready to do whatever was necessary to reclaim my life.

What I didn't know when I boarded the Greyhound that took me from Comstock back to Buffalo is that my freedom would be so short-lived. Forty days later, I would be back in custody, charged with a crime that would lead the judge in the case to eventually say: "I have never seen or heard of any more ruthless homicides then the three that were committed on these individuals. It is the opinion of this court that you should be removed from society as soon as possible."

You might think that being locked-up in places like Elmira, Coxsackie, and Comstock would have straightened me out. But if you have never been to prison, what is almost impossible to understand is that prisons don't rehabilitate anyone. They are holding pens –places to keep you locked up until they let you loose back into society. You might go in as a stick-up guy. But what do you do? You hang out with drug dealers, loan sharks, arsonists, gangsters, career criminals, rapists and murderers. You go in a bad person and typically come out worse. When released, I had virtually no money, no family to return to, no skills and no conceivable way to earn a living. So I returned to the only life I knew, being a criminal, with the only family I had, the Savage Ones.

It may have taken me 40 days to get arrested, but I had gotten my hands on a gun and committed a robbery within 24 hours of being back in Buffalo. What choice did I have? That was my life and no parole was going to change that.

But to get back to April 23, 1973. We got lots of tips on where to steal stuff. Maybe somebody owed money and couldn't pay. They may ask for a percentage of whatever you steal. They might settle the score by tipping you to a place to rob. This place has antiques, that guy has a gun collection, whatever it might be. That's how we ended up at the house on Olga Place. A tip came in. There was an older couple that had a valuable collection of stamps and coins. Like I said before, cash was king. Easy and untraceable. Stamps, coins, antiques, they all required fencing them out. But still, a valuable haul could be turned around fairly quickly and I figured we could make this hit a decent haul. I needed a partner. You can do a stick-up solo, but a break-in is a two-man job. You need a lookout, and once you are inside, two sets of eyes get the loot and get you out in half the time.

So I ended up pairing up with a fellow Savage One, Tommy. He was 19, a year younger than me, and I knew I could trust him. We had grown up together and had been in prison together. We were both on parole and he was already wanted for other crimes and a parole violation. We had already done a number of burglaries together and had developed a system. We cased the house, for a week before the robbery, figuring out the best way in. There were a couple of false starts. We first planned to hit the house five or six days earlier. It was just around the corner from where I lived, and we walked over and cased the place. But we bailed. We went back the next day and planned to go in then. But again, we backed off. I wish we had found another house, a business, anything that led us away from Olga Place. But we didn't. The lure of what could have been thousands of dollars in coins and stamps on the other side of those clapboard walls was too much to resist. And so, we finalized the plan. We were going in on Monday, April 23. It was the day after Easter and we had heard from our source that the homeowners were going to be in Florida. It should have been an easy in, easy out.

People have asked me, if we thought no one was going to be home, why did we bring guns? Again, to understand that, you have to understand who we were and where we lived. I carried a gun the way a plumber might carry a wrench or a handyman might carry a screwdriver. It was my tool of my trade. The plan was simple: We were going to go in through a window on the side of the house. I would boost Tommy up, and he would shimmy in, come around and let me in the side door. We figured we should be in and out in ten minutes tops. It was a small house and finding the goods shouldn't be too difficult, we thought. We had no idea just how wrong we were.

Chapter 10

We left and began the short walk over to 18 Olga Place just before midnight. The plan was to pawn the coins and stamps the next day.

We didn't wear disguises or masks, none of that. Who the hell was going to see us? We never wore them because we really didn't care if anyone saw us. It was after midnight on a weeknight. The entire neighborhood was asleep. We crept along the house and when we got to the window, I gave Tommy a boost. He pulled off the screen and lifted the window. We were in, nice and clean. We began to check out the house. We were coming for the coins and stamps, but we would take anything that looked like it had value and that we thought we could unload easily. Then, we heard a noise. You already know what happened. The couple didn't go to Florida. They were asleep in their bedrooms and they woke up when they heard us rifling through the front of the house. I don't want to get into what happened next, because it isn't what this book is about. But when we left the house, both of them were dead, shot in the head.

We got what we came for and we headed out the front door. But we weren't free and clear yet. It turned out that a relative lived in an apartment in the rear of the house. He had heard the gunshots and came to investigate. We killed him also. We took off running down Olga, but we came back. I checked the body as he lay on the ground, and I emptied his pockets. Then we took off running toward the railroad tracks. Someone had heard the shots and called the cops. Sirens were screaming and cop cars were everywhere.

****

Although things happened that we never saw coming, we formed an immediate plan. Hit the tracks, find a place to hide the guns and valuables and then get back on the street. That way, if the cops stop us, we've got nothing on us, no weapons, nothing. They can question us, but they would have to let us go.

So we did it. We dumped everything under a house and five minutes later we were being questioned by the police. They said we matched the description of two guys who had just robbed a house on Olga. They patted us down and put us in the back of the cruiser and drove over to Olga Place, back to the house. What we didn't know was that a neighbor had seen us leaving the house. She watched our confrontation with the man in the yard and she watched him get shot. The police knew. And so, when they brought us back to the house, they pulled us out of the car and stood us right under the streetlight. We didn't know it, but she was in her house, identifying us as the killers. It had been less than two hours since we were sitting in my house, getting ready for what should have been just another break-in. Now, we were cuffed, placed into the back of a police car, and taken to the station to be charged with three counts of murder. Standing there, outside 18 Olga Place, at 1:30 in the morning on April 24, 1973, I took my last breath as a free man. Or so I thought. More than 34 years later, I would receive an unheard of second chance at life. But I had to go to hell and back before that day would come, and as we drove away from Olga Place,

the bodies of our victims still in their house, that journey began.

Chapter 11

It would take 14 months for our trial to occur and for the jury to find me guilty of 11 counts in the 14-count indictment handed down. Most of the experience was a blur. I was guilty, but I didn't help my cause. I refused to cut my hair, which I wore long and straggly, refused to dress properly for court and I would often face away from the judge, and generally act disrespectfully toward the court. No matter how much my lawyer tried to explain that my life was on trial, I ignored him. My actions were those of a 20-year-old kid who cared about no one and nothing, especially myself. In my eyes, my conviction and presumed life sentence were inevitable and so I sat and watched it unfold before my eyes.

When I was arrested for the robbery that first sent me to prison in 1970, I made an idiotic attempt to escape during one of my early court proceedings. They had me handcuffed to another guy, so I don't know what we thought we were going to do, but we ran. Try blending in as you run down Delaware Avenue in downtown Buffalo handcuffed to another man. Needless to say, we were quickly captured, but that "escape" followed me for the next 37 years. Every prison I was in, I was labeled a flight risk. Every time I was transported to court, or to another prison, it was under the watchful eye of armed guards who were ordered to shoot if they so much as saw me attempting to manipulate the cuffs or leg irons that chained me to the seat. Forget that I wasn't a *real* flight risk. A single impulsive act would haunt me. It was a bit of a theme of my life, and one it would take me decades to shake.

The judge in my case, Hon. James Kane, showed no leniency for me, or for my co- defendant Tommy. One thing I try to teach young people when I speak about my crime is the complexities of the legal system. When you commit a crime, it isn't like they charge you with a single crime. The prosecutors pile on as many different charges as possible, hoping to convict you on everything. But really, it is about creating leverage for a plea deal, and also giving them fallback charges in case some don't stick.

In my case, I was indicted by a grand jury in 1973 of fourteen felony charges. They were:

- Murder, for causing the death of XXXXXXXXXXXXXXX
- Murder, for causing the death of XXXXXXXXXXXXXXXX
- Murder, for causing the death of XXXXXXXXXXXXXXXXX
- Murder, for causing the death of XXXXXXXXXXXXXXX, while engaged in the commission of a burglary
- Murder, for causing the death of XXXXXXXXXXXXXXX, while engaged in the commission of a burglary
- Murder, for causing the death of XXXXXXXXXXXXXX, while engaged in the commission of a burglary

- First degree burglary, that resulted in the death of XXXXXXXXXXXXXXXX
- First degree burglary, involving the use of deadly weapons, two revolvers
- First degree burglary, involving displaying firearms during the commission of the robbery.
- Murder, while in the commission of a robbery, for causing the death of XXXXXXXXXXXXXXX in flight from the robbery
- First degree robbery, for stealing XXXXXXXXXXXXXXX wallet from his body while causing serious physical injury
- First degree robbery, for stealing XXXXXXXXXXXXXX wallet while armed with two loaded revolvers
- First degree robbery, for stealing XXXXXXXXXXXXXXX wallet, while displaying what appeared to be firearms

- Possession of a weapon as a convicted felon, for being in possession of a revolver while out on parole from my prior robbery conviction

As I stand in front of an auditorium of wide-eyed students, this is a tough concept to explain to them. The way the system is set-up, we faced seven counts of murder for murdering three people. We took one wallet, yet faced three felonies for taking the same wallet. I'm not bemoaning my situation. I have steadfastly said that I was guilty and deserved the sentence that was eventually imposed on me, but what I do try to do, is show young people the incredibly grave consequences of making poor choices. Steal a wallet and face a felony charge. Steal a wallet while in possession of a gun or knife, face two felonies. Steal a wallet, while in possession of a weapon, and injure the person you are robbing, face three felonies. The legal system is incredibly complex and it isn't set-up for the typical defendant to understand.

My case was a perfect example of why prosecutors stack charges. During the course of the proceedings, the judge dismissed indictment's seven, nine, 11, and 13. That still left ten felony indictments, more than enough to lock us away for the rest of our lives.

When I speak to groups, I simply say, "I killed three people in a robbery." I say it now, and my lawyer argued it at the trial, because it is fact. My co-defendant Tommy was convicted on all 10 felony counts that remained. My jury found me not guilty of the first three counts, all involving the direct murder of the three victims.

That doesn't mean I was innocent. By leveling seven murder charges against me, I was still convicted of four counts of murder, stemming from the murders occurring during the commission of both a burglary and a robbery. Had the prosecutor simply charged me with three counts of murder and left it at that, the jury may have convicted my co-defendant and found me not guilty.

Either way, Judge Kane didn't mince words when he described our crimes as among the worst he had ever seen or heard of. New York State did not allow for capital punishment, and so I was sentenced to 50-years to life with the recommendation that I never be released. As I was led from the courtroom in June, 1974, I fully expected to die in prison. I was 22-years-old.

****

During my trial I had been held at the Erie County Holding Center in downtown Buffalo. While it might not have been the most pleasant place in the world, it was a country club compared to where I was going. Attica Correctional Facility is located in a sleepy, rural town of 7,000 people in the farmlands 30 miles east of Buffalo. The prison, filled with some of the most violent, high-risk prisoners in the country, stood in stark contrast to the working-class people who lived quiet lives in a community where everyone knew their neighbor and crime was virtually non-existent.

There are many who know nothing about prisons and claim they are country clubs because they hear about certain prisons where politicians, lawyers, and other people who have stolen millions of dollars go. Their crimes are usually considered white collar and are federal and that system is different. The kind of prisons they are sent to are totally different than the ones I was sent to. Not once during my 37 plus years of incarceration did I ever play golf, go swimming, or play tennis. I always served what they call "hard time."

I was tough on the streets of East Buffalo, a Savage One, but I doubted that would carry much weight in Attica. I was arriving at the maximum security prison just three years after the Attica Riot, where prisoners took over the prison for four days to protest overcrowding and poor treatment by the guards. When the riot ended, after State Police stormed the prison at the order of then-New York Governor Nelson Rockefeller, 43 people were dead, both prisoners and employees of the prison.

Attica is nothing today like it was back in 1974 when I arrived. There is so much more oversight in the prison system and civil rights groups that look out to make sure prisoners are being treated humanely. But in 1974 I knew I was walking into the middle of a prison that was still massively overcrowded, with a virtual race war going on inside the prison walls between the blacks (who make up the majority), the whites, and the Puerto Ricans. So I did what I had done for my entire life: I developed a survival plan. I knew I had to establish myself within the prison if I was going to make it. The quickest way to do that is to let people know you aren't somebody to be messed with. So my plan was simple. On my first day in general population, I was going to kill someone in the yard. It didn't matter who, it didn't have to be anyone I knew or had a beef with, it just had to be quick and violent and let every person in that prison know, you mess with Jerry Balone and this is what will happen.

I had a few weeks of processing when I arrived at Attica – standard stuff before you get placed into general population, so I had time to get my hands on a weapon. It's funny what people think about prison life and how much public perception differs from reality. People think that because there are guards, and security, because the mail is read and the visitors are searched, that prisons are safe places. Nothing could be further from the truth, especially back in the 1970s. Attica was like a black market Wal-Mart in the 1970s. Drugs, alcohol, food, weapons, cigarettes, sex, gambling, clothing, cash, you name it, and for a price, it could be yours. Back then, the guards couldn't care less what we did to one another as long as we didn't do anything to them. As long as we weren't trying to escape, it was all a game. Guards know everything that goes on within a prison and it was advantageous to them to have the prisoners hating one another instead of worrying about and making problems about the horrible conditions that exist in prisons across the country. Then there was the fact that you've got a lot of smart prisoners. Not book smart, but cunning. You give a guy 24 hours a day to think and he will come up with things you've never even imagined in your wildest dreams. So getting a weapon was easy. I then planned to slide the shiv up my arm of my shirt and head into the yard. I wasn't wasting any time. I was going to stick the first person that looked at me.

The day I was cleared for my first trip to the yard, my adrenaline was soaring. I was like a kid at Christmas I was so amped up to get out there and establish myself. For me, it was the first step toward settling in for what I expected to be a lifetime in Attica. At that time, I had no idea that they would routinely reassign me to a new prison, shipping me out anytime they thought I was becoming too popular, or too connected. I had no clue that I would serve time in 17 prisons in New York State. I was still a kid, and I was naive enough to believe I would spend the rest of my life in Attica, so for me, it was time to mark my territory.

But then, a funny thing happened. Decades later I would look back and clearly see that this was the hand of God reaching down to intervene, but at the time, God was nothing to me and so I made no such connection. As I walked toward the doors to take me into the yard, which was packed with maybe 400 prisoners getting their daily recreation, I had the prison shiv flat against my arm, concealed in my shirt. I could feel the sweat running down my back and small beads of perspiration forming on my brow. I was so ready. The doors swung open and as I stepped out and began to survey for my victim, I heard someone yell my name. "Jerry!" Then another and another, and another. Before I had time to acclimate to my surroundings, I had prisoners lining up, slapping me on the back, hugging me, and welcoming me to Attica. The thing is, I had grown up in the system. I was arrested for the first time when I was eight-years-old. My mother had abandoned me at the hospital and I had bounced around from foster homes, orphanages, detention centers, and reform schools. Sometimes a judge would send me back to live with my mother, but I would eventually run away, until I got caught and put back into juvenile hall, or sent to reform schools like Berkshire Farms and Industry. So, on that hot summer day, in the yard at the Attica Correctional Facility, it was somewhat of a homecoming for me. It was like a class reunion of every troubled kid I had grown up with. Over the next few days, I would come to realize I knew more than 200 of the people who were in the yard that day. So, I didn't have to kill anybody. I had the credentials I needed to survive, and I quickly found that I had the makings of a new family – my prison family.

Chapter 12

I entered the prison system with roughly a fifth-grade education. And it wasn't much of an education. Most of the time I was being bounced from school to school because of behavior issues or I was being sent to juvenile hall, foster homes, an orphanage, and reform schools. When I was in school, I didn't pay attention, didn't study and didn't care. You find that a lot in prisons. They are places filled with incredibly frustrated people who are angry and lashing out. I'm not saying it all traces back to education, but the lack of education among the prisoners certainly contributes to how many of them end up in prison and it absolutely makes it more challenging to survive on the inside and get out quicker – or stay out when you're released.

If you go into the prisons here today, the college programs are gone. When times got tough on the outside, the politicians cut the funding for college on the inside. The logic was something like this: Why waste money on those deadbeats when there are law-abiding people out here in need. Well, speaking from experience, I can say without a doubt, without the education I received in prison, I would still be incarcerated. The taxpayers would be spending $35,000 or more yearly to house me, feed me and care for me. Instead, not only are they not paying that expense, but I am out here working, paying taxes and contributing to society. The state made an investment in me, and that investment is paying dividends. The decision to cut funding for education in prisons was short-sighted, and I am living proof that the programs they had in place worked.

Education programs inside not only offered hope to the prisoners who participated, but they also acted as a check and balance within a prison. Prisoners like getting out of their cells. One of the hardest parts of surviving prison is the mind-numbing boredom. Your day is so regimented and there is rarely, if ever, any change in the routine. School was one of those rare changes. If I wanted to get to go to class, to escape the doldrums, then I best stay clean. No fights, no contraband, nothing. The promise of going to school kept a lot of the prisoners in line, and if you've ever been inside of a prison, then you know, keeping order is both the most important thing, and often the most difficult.

For the first 15 or more years of my incarceration, I was ruthless. I ran drugs. I gambled. I worked as a loan shark and a bookie. And along with that, if you didn't pay when you owed, I took care of you. People didn't mess with me because they knew what would happen. It wasn't some tough-guy talk or some idle threat, they knew.

I can't remember when it happened, but I recall all of us received a memo from the prison administration where I was locked up telling us that we would no longer be called prisoners, convicts or any of those other so-called negative names. Also, prisons would no longer be called prisons. They would now be called "correctional facilities," and we would be called "inmates." Absolutely nothing changed as far as treatment. Many of us refused to embrace the title of "inmate" and as far as I was concerned, I was still a convicted felon and a prisoner being held against his will. I was the ultimate prisoner and convict!

Then one day, something happened that changed my life forever.

I got word that I was being transferred again. This time they were sending me to Shawangunk Correctional Facility. It is a SuperMax facility located in Wallkill, New York, roughly halfway between New York City and Albany. The prison was built in 1985, completed in 1986, and it became my home shortly thereafter. By now, I was used to being moved around. I never cared where they sent me because I didn't get visits and it broke up the boredom of prison life. I was street smart and prison smart so I knew I'd survive in whatever prison they sent me to. There are 16 maximum-security prisons in New York State. I've served time in 12 of them, some of them more than once. I began my sentence in Attica in 1974 and was paroled from Fishkill in 2007. In between I served time in Auburn, Clinton, Coxsackie, Downstate, Eastern, Elmira, Comstock, Shawangunk, Sing Sing, Sullivan, and Upstate. Once I got moved to medium security facilities I was locked down in Collins, Orleans, Tappan and Woodbourne before ending up in Fishkill, in what would be my final prison.

What I didn't know, was what was in store for me when I arrived in Shawangunk. On my first night in my new cell, I noticed something I had never seen before in any of the other prisons I had been in. There was a camera trained on my cell. It captured every move I made and watched me 24-hours a day. There was no privacy whatsoever. The guards could not only hear everything we were doing, they could see it too. It was a prison within a prison, and even with everything I had been through, it made me uneasy. I had grown naturally distrustful of the guards and of prison in general, and the idea that I was now under constant surveillance was a bit unnerving.

Shortly after arriving at the prison, I was brought into a large area with the 63 other prisoners in that unit. There we were met by a prison official who "welcomed" us to the facility. He proceeded to tell us that we had been selected and deemed to be the 64 most dangerous and disruptive criminals in the New York

State prison system. That was how we ended up in Shawangunk Close Supervision Unit (CSU) located in B-2. He informed us that they really didn't care what we did to each other. We could kill each other for all they cared, but they would do what was necessary to restore and keep order in the prison. But it was what he said next that caught my ear.

"Each of you will have the opportunity to work your way out of this unit," he told us. Having imagined what it would be like to live under the constant scrutiny of a camera, I already knew I wanted out, so I listened. He told us that there were educational opportunities at Shawangunk as well as chances to volunteer and do other therapeutic programs. If we took advantage of those opportunities, we could someday be returned to the general population of the prison or be transferred to another one. I knew immediately that I was going to do whatever it took to get out of Shawangunk as fast as I could. Little did I know that I would end up spending over five years in that prison.

Besides being a convicted murderer, I was a con man, a liar, a thief, and a hustler. It was what I had done my entire life and for me, this was nothing more than a challenge to put a lifetime of skills to the test. They thought they were smart. I knew I was smarter.

As I've said, there is a deeply rooted subculture in prison. There is a black market where you can have anything—for a price. Sometimes that price is money, oftentimes it is cigarettes, and it can be sex, food, anything that another prisoner wants, becomes barter for goods. When I first began my sentence, I got into the drug game. It was a lucrative business and I was good at it. In the 1970s, it was relatively easy to run a drug operation in prison. The guards really didn't care what we were doing and getting the stuff in the door was much easier than it is today. You got a girl on the outside to visit and bring your stuff in. She could fill her bra, her panties, wherever she could. Then, once she got inside, it was easy to slip the stuff to a prisoner. But eventually, there was too much violence associated with the drug trade and the administration started to crack down. When I first arrived, if you got caught with drugs, they would put you in solitary for a few weeks; take away some privileges and that was about it. But when they wanted to get a handle on the violence, the rules suddenly changed. Now, if you got caught with drugs, you were charged the same way you would be on the outside and it meant a trial and added time along with being placed in solitary for years with loss of good time and other privileges. Trust me when I say that today, drugs are still a huge problem in the prison system. There are still plenty of prisoners with nothing to lose, or who don't care about anything, who are willing to get high and deal to support their habit. But I wasn't, and so that's when I decided to get out of that game and I turned to gambling.

Like I said, prison is an incredibly boring place. One of the biggest ways prisoners pass the time is by gambling. Football, ponies, handball, horses, basketball, baseball, political elections, the weather, you name it, and there would be somebody who wanted action on it. While they began cracking down on drugs, the guards generally looked the other way on gambling. It was considered no big deal. It kept the the prison high. So it was allowed to go on, and I made enough to live well in prison. I had most anything I wanted on the inside.

It was also impossible to run any kind of illegal enterprise under 24-hour video monitoring. So I knew if I was going to take care of my business, I had to get out from under the surveillance in Shawangunk. If that meant faking my way through some educational and therapeutic programs with other prisoners, then that's what I would do.

And so I did. It was 1989 and I began taking classes at Ulster County Community College. Professors would come from the college and we had the same books and curriculum as the students on campus. I didn't have much of an education up to that point. When I was a kid and started to get in trouble and act out, they had me tested. Somebody, a doctor, a shrink - assigned by the state - was paid to talk to me - said I was mentally retarded. At the age of eight, I was unable to count to ten and did not know my ABCs because no one had ever sat down and taught them to me. I do remember, I wore that diagnosis like a badge of honor. I would sit in the back of the class (when I actually went to school) and when the teachers would call on me for my homework, I would tell them, I don't do home work, I'm a retard. Eventually, most of the teachers stopped asking, and I just sort of existed in school, until I mostly stopped going all together.

So the idea of working to earn a college degree was a joke to me. I was doing it for all the wrong reasons, and I didn't think I would even make it through the program. Even though I was a grown man, I still heard the little kid inside me saying, I'm a retard. I had been told for so long that I was retarded, that I was never going to amount to anything, that eventually, I believed it. It would take years of education and counseling and self-exploration to realize I was better than what those people had said and I was better than I even believed, but back then, as I walked in to attend my first college class, I still saw myself as an uneducated retard.

I've said that it was getting transferred to Shawangunk that changed my life, and it did. Were it not for the intensive monitoring I was going to have to live under, I would never have considered taking the educational programs as a way out. If I had never agreed to sign up for the classes, I would not have found out the most incredible thing: I like to learn. I had been convinced by so many people that there was something wrong with me, that I just assumed it was true. But it wasn't. One thing about prison, you talk to a lot of counselors. You go through a lot of mental evaluations. It turned out, I never was retarded. I didn't have all of the psychological problems other people said that I had. Sure, I had issues. I came from a home where my mother abandoned me and I never knew my father. We grew up poor and I lived a life I wouldn't wish on my worst enemy. I developed anger issues and issues dealing with authority figures, but I didn't have any kind of retardation or a learning disability like they said. At the age of 37, I began taking my first college courses, I couldn't get enough. It was like my brain was a sponge that hadn't been used in years and I was soaking up everything. Soon, I began to read everything I could get my hands on. I wanted to study psychology and sociology—a fitting course of study given my surroundings, and so I often chose books from similar areas. Before long, I was lugging books with me everywhere I went: studying, reading and doing homework.

The deeper I got into the program; I quickly realized I didn't want to lose the privilege to go to classes. So I began to be more careful about my behavior. The guards were always watching and I knew the slightest violation, and they would yank me out of college. That's how they operate a prison. Find what's important to you, and dangle it over you to keep you in line. If you're one of the lucky few who get visitors, that fact becomes leverage for the guards to keep you in line. You like receiving mail? Enjoy getting out of your cell and sitting in class, escaping the monotony of prison life? Then you best follow every rule and not even think of slipping up. This reality created a serious problem for me in my prison existence.

On one hand, I was 18 years into my stretch and I had earned a reputation in the prison system. I was an earner, a hustler and most of all I was someone you didn't mess with. Now, with me taking on college, there were grumblings among some of my fellow prisoners. They wondered if I was getting soft. Because the prison system is built on a system of snitches, this is a big deal. Anytime someone is caught breaking the rules –whether it is for having contraband in their cell, fighting, sneaking food, selling or possessing drugs, stealing, whatever it is, they are given the chance to flip. Offer a bigger fish, and the guards might let you go, or at least lessen your punishment. So the idea that Jerry Balone might somehow be going over to the other side had people worried. The few people who had the balls to ask me to my face if I was going soft got the same answer: You think I'm getting soft. Try me and find out. No one ever did.

And so it was that I began to earn an education. I quickly found it to be addicting. What began as a way to beat the system and get a transfer out of Shawangunk, led me to a path that I have enjoyed ever since. My life was slowly beginning to change, although I still never expected to ever be released. You don't murder three people and ever get paroled. It just doesn't happen. But I continued to work at my education, supplementing it with taking every available therapeutic program the prisons offered.

It was the same with the therapeutic programs. I started attending Alternatives to Violence to impress the administration and was asked by the outside people to become a facilitator in that program. It was the first time in my life that I had been asked to join something that wasn't illegal. I met so many wonderful volunteers from the free world and got to meet and interact with lots of prisoners in the system.

I always had the respect of other prisoners. In a culture dominated by race wars, socioeconomic wars and turf battles, I always managed to command the respect of most of them. Part of it was fear –fear of me because of the nature of my crime. Part of it was the way I conducted myself on the inside. In 37 years in the system, I never ratted out a single person. My word was gold. If you gambled and won, I paid you. If I owed you something, you got it. When a new prisoner would arrive, if he was a friend or a friend of a friend, I always made sure he had a welcome package to hold him over till he got on his feet: Toiletries, snacks, coffee, creamer, sugar, soap, a bucket, shower slippers, cigarettes, mirror, reading materials and a few comforts to help him ease into the prison until he was able to get his own property or make it to the commissary. In the twisted subculture of prison, I was a stand-up guy.

The respect was a double-edged sword. I was also respected because people knew if you owed me and didn't pay, I would come find you. Like I said, we would settle the debt in a stairwell and you would end up in the infirmary. It wasn't pretty and I'm not proud of many of the things I did while in prison, but it is a war inside and you do what you have to do to survive.

Now, I was suddenly finding the respect coming from a different direction. People saw what I was doing, saw that I was trying to turn my life around, and there was a respect there as well. For the first time in my life, people were looking up to me for something that wasn't violent or illegal. It was a different feeling, something I had never experienced before, and I liked it. Over the coming years, as my education flourished, I became a leader in educational and therapeutic programs in the prison system. Soon I was leading programs to assist other prisoners in their educational and rehabilitation efforts. After years of living my life on the inside in the same reckless, violent manner in which I had existed on the outside, I was slowly changing. Through my education, I began to accept responsibility for what I had done –not just the murders, but everything I had done in my life. Whether or not I ever earned my release from prison, I had turned the corner and moved increasingly far from the 20-year-old punk who entered the system back in 1974.

Fast approaching 40-years-old and for the first time in my entire life, I began to see some value in me. I had things to offer people, contributions to make and opportunities to atone for my crimes. I could never bring back my victims no matter how much I wish I could. But I began to see that I could work hard, harder than anybody, to take my experiences, my horrible choices, and work to show other people how to change, in the hopes I might save other people from following the path I took in my life. And I owed it all to my prison education.

Chapter 13

When I talk to groups –primarily students—about my life, I do so with a single purpose: To help people who are struggling to avoid making the same mistakes I made. After decades of healing through studying, reading, and counseling, I've come to understand my life and how I ended up where I did. For many of today's young people, they don't have that luxury of obtaining an education like I was able to acquire. And the pressure on today's kids is far greater than I had growing up in the 1960s. Well, maybe it isn't greater, but it is certainly more in-their-face. We never had to contend with the internet, social media, cell phones and the instantaneous peer pressure that collectively comes with all of those.

Having said this, my life roots were established long-before technology would have had an impact on my life development. The reality was, my roots grew from a diseased family tree and grew out of control. Every poor choice I made added more fertilizer to the roots and anchored my life deeper in the mess.

I was born on November 15, 1952 in Lackawanna, NY. My mother had a hard-luck life. She was a strikingly beautiful woman, but like so many of us, she opted for poor choices in her personal life. I have never known who my father was for the simple fact that I don't believe my mother even knew. She was a raging alcoholic and many nights she would go into a local bar, and whoever bought her the most drinks could take her home and do whatever they wanted to her. I'm sure I was conceived during one of these drunken bar room trysts, and thus never had my father around. My mother ended up having six children (three girls and three boys) with five different men. I'm the only one who ended up in prison but all of them still suffer from the effects of our childhood. I regularly see two of my sisters and one brother. The other sister I haven't seen in over 40 years and I saw my other brother, once, since I've been out of prison. None of us are married or in any type of meaningful relationship.

The City of Buffalo today it is estimated that 60 percent of the homes are occupied by single mothers. Some people call it an epidemic. I don't know about that, but I do know that whatever it was, my mother had no interest in having another child and that mindset put into motion a series of events that shaped my life.

What it does make me is an expert at, is being able to tell you that: no matter what happens in your life, it isn't an excuse for your behavior. Sure, maybe it is when you are a young child. But by the time I was a teenager, I knew right from wrong, I just didn't care. I had evolved into a selfish, self-centered kid who figured the world owed me something. Forget that my mother abandoned me in the hospital when I was born. Forget that when the court tracked her down and forced her to take me back, I endured years of physical and psychological abuse until I ran away so often and got into so much trouble, the authorities finally put me into a string of foster homes, an orphanage , juvenile detention, and reform schools. Forget it all. I knew what the right thing was to do. I knew it was wrong to steal. I knew it was wrong to rob people and vandalize property. But I lived by my own rules and I ended up paying for it in the end.

Please don't misunderstand me. I know a lot of you who are reading this have endured similar hardships to mine and - for some of you - things that are and were even worse. I know some of you have children or other relatives who are currently incarcerated, or at least heading down that road. I am absolutely not trying to minimize your experiences or those of the ones you love. What I am trying share with you is, there are other options.

I played the blame game. I blamed my mother. I blamed my nameless, faceless father. I blamed the nuns and priests in the orphanages that beat me, convinced that I was possessed by the Devil. I blamed the police, the courts, my teachers, foster parents, hell, I even blamed my victims. If I stuck you up and stole your money, it was your fault. Who walks out of a bank in broad daylight with an envelope full of cash? You were asking for it.

The problem with the blame game is that no one cares. There is a saying I like a lot: You can make excuses or you can make a difference, but you can't make both. For the first 40 years of my life, I made excuses. And what did those excuses get me? They got me to spend most of my life institutionalized. Only when I began to study, and started to see options, did I quit making excuses and begin to make a difference, first in my own life, and then in the lives of others around me. If you take one message away from reading my story, let it be that one. The sooner you stop making excuses for yourself, or someone you love, the faster you can begin to heal, grow and make a difference of your own.

I was speaking to a group of students in Pennsylvania in 2011 and during a break in the presentation, a woman approached me. She wanted to share the story of her son. He was in his 20s and had been in prison already. Now, he was living at home with her and getting in all kinds of trouble. She was confident he was going to end up back in jail, or worse, dead. She wanted my advice. He wouldn't listen to her, refused to follow the rules of the house, and was doing illegal things. As she told me each thing her son was doing, the narrative included an excuse. He stayed out late because he was with friends. He refused to listen to her because he was frustrated because he couldn't find a job. The excuses began to pile up. I politely listened, and when she was done, I offered my advice as she had requested.

You need to put him out on the street, I told her. Her face dropped. She stared back at me, mouth agape, unsure of what to say. So I repeated myself. You need to get him out of your house before he hurts you or someone in your family (she has four other children living at home). I explained to her that if he was unwilling to accept responsibility for himself, there was nothing she could do for him. In fact, she was simply enabling him by allowing him to stay in her home and continually make excuses for him. It was time for tough love, and maybe putting him out would be the jolt he needed to wake up, stop making excuses and start making a difference.

Just then, the facilitator signaled me that it was time to resume my talk. I handed the woman my business card and told her it was going to be tough, but if she loved her son, she needed to put him out and he would either sink or swim, but she had a responsibility to herself and the rest of her family to make sure that if he sank, he didn't pull them down with him.

It is a difficult concept for anyone to grasp, but until we can stop making excuses, we can't hope to begin making a difference, at least a true, lasting difference.

My ability to accept the past and begin to focus on the future didn't come overnight. It wasn't like I walked out of that first college class back in 1989 and a lifetime of anger, hatred, violence and despair suddenly melted away. It took me years to reach a place in my life where I could truly look ahead and stop focusing on the "what-ifs" in my life and stop playing the blame game.

But eventually I did. I knew it was the only way I was going to survive. Sure, I could go on existing for the rest of my life, gradually growing more jaded, bitter and entitled until I grew old and died, blaming everyone for my problems right up till the end. But I wasn't content to survive, I wanted to thrive. I wanted to fulfill what I saw as a destiny. I wanted to make a difference in the world and so I did what it took to dig deep and fight past a lifetime of abuse, to climb over a mountain of hatred and stand on top to declare that I was no longer going to see myself as a victim, constantly blaming others. Instead, I was going to shake off the shackles of my past, leave it all behind and build the life I wanted for myself.

****

The problem with planning to change is that people in your life know your history. In my case, I was a thief, a liar, a hoodlum and a murderer. Prison is full of people who "find God" when it is convenient, or miraculously decide to turn over a new leaf when it is time to get ready for a parole hearing. The prison officials have seen it all and are rightfully suspicious. At first, no matter how many classes I took or programs I participated in, I was still nothing more than prisoner No. 74C0264, a murderer who was also a flight risk.

But I didn't care because I was beginning to develop a vision for my life, the plan that would eventually spring me from the hell on Earth that had been my life. It is another of the messages that I bring to the young people I speak to and mentor. You have to want it bad enough. You hear this often with athletes who suffer a severe injury and have to miss an entire season, going through months of painful rehabilitation to return to play. No longer are they playing in front of 60,000 screaming fans on Sunday. Instead, they are far removed from the spotlight. They are in a weight room, or a doctor's office working tirelessly, fighting through the pain and depression of the situation, determined not to give up until they make it back. Now you might say, 'Sure, but they have a million dollar career waiting for them when they make it back.' Therein lays the problem. Isn't your life worth more than money? If they can work so hard, train, fight, bleed, do whatever it takes to get back on top, doesn't your life mean enough to make it worth fighting for? If it doesn't right now, you are like I was in 1988. I saw no hope, no purpose, and no chance to be anything more than the common thug I had always been. It was only after I had begun to make the changes in my life, and saw more hope for a better life than I could have ever dreamed up, that I was willing to do whatever it took, for no matter how long it took, to rebuild my life.

I took that first college class in 1989. It would be 18 years, more than 6,000 days and nights later before I would walk free. But I never gave up, I never gave in and I never backed down. Once I knew what I wanted –my life back—nothing was going to stop me and no price was too high to pay. If you aren't there yet in your life, I hope and pray for you that you get there. It is a glorious place to be, knowing that you will do whatever it takes to succeed, because when you have that mindset, it becomes a matter of when, not if, you will create the life of your dreams.

Chapter 14

Just because I had turned a corner in my life, didn't mean it was smooth sailing. I still lived in a cell, locked away from the rest of the world. Most of the food I ate, you wouldn't feed to a dog: and I existed in an isolation that breaks many men.

I had not been with a woman in more than 20 years. I hadn't been intimate since I was a teenager. Lots of guys on the inside have women who visit them. Some are wives or girlfriends who have decided to stick by their men. Those are usually the ones serving relatively short sentences, where their significant other has some hope of reuniting and at least pretending there will be a fairytale ending.

I was a triple murderer who stood a million-to-one odds of ever being released. Who would want to visit me? I really didn't care all that much about what was going on out in the free world because that world was totally different than the one I was living in and I had no expectations of ever enjoying life on the outside again.

Many of the guys had women visiting them who they had met through pen pal programs or other ways. The women would seek out prisoners and it was a relationship built on mutual manipulation. The con would say all the right things, make the women feel special, maybe even loved, and in return, he got regular visits from someone on the outside, which is gold when you are locked up. Forget what you read about overcrowding, prison can be the loneliest place on Earth. The feelings of isolation can be unbearable for a lot of the men, and so a woman, no matter what she might look like, who is willing to come for regular visits, is a sought after commodity. Not to mention that most of the visiting rooms had soda and food machines and visitors could bring in money. If you eat prison food seven days a week, suddenly frozen hamburgers zapped in a microwave and a cold can of Coke feels like you are eating caviar and sipping champagne.

Those benefits notwithstanding, I still had no real interest in having women visit me. I had opportunities. Guys had relatives, or friends, or even friends of the girls that were visiting them. But what was I supposed to talk about with them? I had no life before I went to prison. I had nothing to say to anyone and no ability to hold a decent conversation with a woman if I tried. I had met a few women that visited but all ended in failure. That all changed when I met Christine.

It was 1993 and I had been transferred to Sullivan Correctional Facility. Sullivan is a maximum security prison about 100 miles north of New York City. Like many of the prisons I've been locked up in, it was in a rural setting, in a small town called Fallsburg. Sullivan wasn't the worst prison I had ever been in, but it was far from the best. It was however, the place where I met Christine. She had come to Sullivan to visit someone else, but we sort of crossed paths in the visiting room, and maybe there was a spark. I don't really know what else to call it. I had never had a real relationship in my life, so it is tough for me to say what the connection was. But, it was enough for Christine to begin to write to me, and to visit.

By now, I had made so much progress with my education and my therapeutic programs, in many ways; I was a million miles from the man I was when the door first closed behind me in Attica back in 1974. I had grown emotionally, intellectually and spiritually so far that it was sometimes hard for me to fathom what I had done in my life. I had so much regret. I knew I had caused so much pain that could never be erased in so many people's lives. I knew seeking forgiveness was futile, but I really wanted people to see that I wasn't the same person who entered the prison system back in 1974. It didn't lessen my crime, or make me any less responsible, but I truly *had* been trying to atone for my crimes –for my life really, and maybe that's why I was willing to let my guard down and let someone else get close to me.

Christine was amazing. She was one of the first people who really believed in me. There were teachers, counselors, professors, religious people, and others who saw value in me and believed I was working to change my life, but Christine was the first person who truly saw me as a man first, and a murderer second. In fact, I'm not sure she saw me as a murderer at all. To her, I was someone to be judged on my actions now, not my life as a whole.

Christine had a rough life too. She had been in her fair share of abusive relationships and had been diagnosed with polio. Though I never use it as an excuse, life had dealt me some tough cards and in that way, Christine and I had some things in common, and it was a connection between us.

During this time, I was working hard to prepare to convince a parole board to set me free. When I was originally sentenced in 1974, I received 50 years to life with the recommendation that I never be released. But in the early 1990s, the courts declared my sentence and thousands of others to be illegal. One day I woke up in my cell, expecting to be in my seventies before I was even eligible for parole. Then, a letter arrived telling me that my sentence had been reduced to 25 years to life. Just like that, my sentence was cut in half. Even though I had earned all of my degrees and taken advantage of every program available, I knew they would never let me go. But once I met Christine, she was my first advocate on the outside. She would write letters on my behalf: call officials, lobby for my release. She would explore every avenue and search for ways to improve my chances to earn my freedom.

It felt strange to have someone fighting for me like that. Having come from a home where my mother left me at the hospital and my father was nonexistent, I never had anyone really looking out for me. Having spent my entire life fending for myself, it felt strange to be able to count on someone else.

People often ask me, what kind of women falls for a guy in prison, especially a guy who did what you did and was probably never getting out? In Christine's case, having suffered through multiple abusive relationships, she found a man who couldn't abuse her. I was locked away. Maybe that made her feel safe. Or, maybe, after her four marriages had failed, she thought this was the best she could do. I really don't know what her motivation was, though I suspect it was a combination of things. What I do know now is that our relationship was doomed to fail. It's hard enough to make it work for people living on the outside, but imagine the pressure of trying to make things work under the circumstances we faced. Once we began to officially "date" Christine would come to visit me on the weekends or whenever she could. I was transferred to several different prisons during our time together, and some of those trips would entail her driving more than 1,000 miles round-trip to see me.

I had nothing to offer her in the beginning. We couldn't share intimate moments, or even private moments for that matter. I've seen some couples who were married and then the guy goes to prison and the relationship is able to survive. But they had a history before he got locked up. With Christine and me, she became obsessed with helping me earn my parole. I think in her mind, she saw a life where I was released and we rode off into the sunset to live happily ever after. It was what kept us both going. It is what kept her writing letters, kept her driving those long miles to visit, kept her believing in me.

Eventually, I was transferred to Elmira Correctional Facility. Elmira is a rural place set in the Finger Lakes region of Western New York. It's a beautiful place to visit—unless of course you're locked up. It was there that I did something I never expected to do in my entire life. I married Christine. We got married in August of 2000. We had been "seeing" each other for four years and now we were husband and wife. Deep in my heart, I think I knew it wasn't going to work, but we pushed ahead.

Though we would eventually divorce, in the years that followed our marriage, she was my number one advocate. I was working day and night on the inside to win my release and she was doing the same on the outside. We were a great team. I wrote letters every day. To politicians, clergy, whoever I thought might listen. I knew I was fighting long odds to earn my freedom. Outside, Christine was doing the same thing. When I met her she was incredibly introverted, almost reclusive. But I worked with her, got her reading the types of books I was reading and trained her to be confident and become a public speaker. It was about the only thing I could give her, but I think it was an important one.

By the time we got married I had already been before the parole board and turned down three times. But we both believed the next time would be different. I was working so hard and I had now earned five college degrees. We also assumed the marriage would look good to the parole board. So many ex-cons leave prison with no one or nothing waiting for them on the outside. A return to prison becomes inevitable without the support network on the outside. With me, I was going to have a wife and a home to return to when I was released. This had to mean something, didn't it? The truth was, it didn't mean a thing. To many of us on the inside who were trying to obtain our freedom, the parole system in New York was and is still considered one of the most unjust organizations in the country. But it is also a group of individuals that wield an incredible amount of unchecked power. Most of the power was used to rubber stamp "denied" across parole applications. The way it worked, if you got denied, it was two years before you were eligible to appear before the board again. Because I had accomplished so much in prison and been a model prisoner for my later years, there wasn't much they could say when they denied me so they always fell back on, "the nature of my crime." Forget the hundreds of letters I had from prominent people in the community urging them to consider me for parole. Forget my own words and my accomplishments. They looked right past it all and hit me with "denied" every time.

It became a routine for me. I would spend every single day preparing for my hearing. I would gather support, write letters and do the hardest part—stay out of trouble. No matter how determined I was to stay on the straight and narrow I was locked in a prison with hundreds of angry, anti-social people. Don't get me wrong, there were a lot of good people in prison, too. A lot of people who got mixed up in drugs or other things and got arrested and convicted. So keeping clean was a challenge. Somebody always wanted to start a beef with you. So I had that pressure to deal with, which I handled. Then I would appear before the board and plead my case. In theory they were supposed to review my file, review my portfolio of accomplishments and support letters and then interview me. From there, they rendered a decision. My contention was, and still is, that those decisions were rendered before they ever walked into the room. But I went through the motions and showed up every two years beginning in 1995, each time getting my hopes up, despite telling myself it was a scam and a set-up.

Eventually, it became too much for Christine to bear. She stuck with me when I was denied parole in 2001, but when I lost my bid in 2003, I think it was just too much for her. She really believed that together, we would get me set free. After the second time she had to watch me be denied (and my fifth time overall), she had had enough. She wanted a divorce and who could blame her? We were also having financial problems because she was living on social security disability and retirement checks and they barely paid the rent. Three years of marriage is tough. Three years of marriage with a man doing what sure seemed like it was a life sentence, well, that was near impossible. I didn't fight it. I wished her well and we quickly and quietly divorced. She remarried after our divorce. Little did either of us know that four years later I would be a free man.

Chapter 15

As I write this book, there are more than 2.2 million adults incarcerated in the United States. Add to that nearly 100,000 juveniles locked up and another 5 million on probation or parole (including me) and its clear there is a serious and fundamental flaw in the justice system in this country. The United States has the highest documented incarcerated rate in the world. In 2010, 743 of every 100,000 adult Americans were locked up.

It's a driving force behind why I wanted to write this book. For some people, I hope my story inspires them. I came from nothing, literally abandoned at birth. I grew up into a petty criminal, a street thug who did what was expected of me. I graduated to bigger and bigger crimes until I was sent to prison, a place many of my teachers, neighbors and victims would have both predicted and welcomed as an outcome. But I never quit and I never gave up. I fought for my life when I was younger and I fought for my freedom as I grew older. Today, I am fighting for both, while working to educate as many young people as possible so that they may benefit from my experiences and avoid following the path my life took me down. So if you or someone you love are able to draw inspiration from my story, then I am blessed.

Others may read this tale as a roadmap of what not to do. You might see me as someone who deserved the death penalty, as someone who at the bare minimum, should be locked away for life. But despite that, you will at the least walk away from this book knowing that you will never do what I have done and end up where I have been. That too, leaves me feeling grateful. If you are wondering how I could feel blessed by people who think I should be locked up, or worse, dead, it stems back to the core of who I am and why I believe God gave me a second chance at life after my family, friends and everyone else had left me for dead long ago.

People don't get convicted of participating in three murders and ever see the light of day again. The chances of me gaining my freedom were a million to one. And yet here I sit, in my home, on my own computer, writing this. I am a free man. I have my own business, a wallet with credit cards, a computer, cell phone and a Facebook account with 5,000 "friends." So why am I free? How did I beat the odds? I truly believe it was God's plan for me. I know that sounds like a cliché. Man goes to prison, finds God and is suddenly redeemed. I can assure you, that's not how I see myself.

First of all, I don't think I am redeemed. Three people are dead because of me and there are families out there living with that pain that I caused. I don't know if I can ever be fully redeemed. I know that I feel an obligation to do whatever I can to atone for my crime and make as much positive as I can out of the tragedy that I participated in. Secondly, I went to prison an atheist and spent much of my incarceration hating God. For me, it was more than not believing in God. I believed in him and hated him for what he had done to me. Growing up and being subjected to regular beatings from the nuns, priests, teachers, counselors, foster parents and others who thought I had the Devil in me didn't help. My mother abandoning me, then when I was returned to her, alternating between ignoring me and systematically abusing me didn't help. Where was God when I needed him? Why would God allow all of the horrible things in my life happen to a little kid? The way I saw it, either there was no God, or he existed, and he was evil. Either way, I spent many years in prison without ever "coming to God." And it wasn't for lack of opportunities. There were church services, chaplains, pamphlets, booklets and bibles available. But I wanted nothing to do with any of it.

It wasn't until many years and many prisons into my incarceration that I came to know God and understand why I had made some of the choices I made in my life and why I was the person I was. I owe my salvation and my relationship with my creator to a group of Dominican nuns in Elmira and Buffalo who had heard about my story and began writing me letters. I met them through Christine who would stay with them when she visited me at Elmira. At first, I wanted nothing to do with them, but eventually, I began to think about some of the things they were telling me. They talked about forgiveness and redemption, and the thing was, I knew my victims' families were never going to forgive me. How could they? But it was one letter they wrote that said, "Jerry, how can you expect other people to forgive you when you can't even forgive yourself?"

In Luke 6:37 it says: "Do not judge and you will not be judged. Do not condemn, and you will not be condemned. Forgive, and you will be forgiven."

I thought about that a lot at night, once the lights were shut down and it was quiet in prison. I had spent a lifetime judging others, and here I was, locked down in the ultimate act of judgment. I had condemned my family, condemned my enemies and condemned complete strangers as I victimized them. And what had I gotten for it in return? Complete and total condemnation. The one thing I had never done was to forgive.

Eventually, I began to pray. I began to talk to God and most importantly, I came to forgive myself for everything in my life. But it wasn't just me. I had to forgive my father who I never knew. I had to forgive the people who had beaten me and the teachers and others who told me I was retarded. I had to forgive my enemies; I had to forgive the guards who had done me wrong. And, in what might be one of the most difficult things I have ever had to do, I had to forgive my mother. Here was the woman who was supposed to love me, to care for me, to do anything in the world to protect me, and she had done just the opposite. I truly believed that I wouldn't be in prison if she had cared for me, and so I held all-consuming hatred in my heart toward her.

But as I began to understand God, and to read the Bible, I came to see that the Dominican Nuns were right. If I was ever going to find peace, if I was ever going to begin to rebuild my life, I had to forgive *everybody*. It may sound quick here as I write it, but the process took me a long time. In fact, it is a work in progress. As I learned, we are all sinners who fall short of the grace of God. As I stand here today, I am far from perfect. And as I began to learn about forgiveness back then, I was a broken fallible man. I worked hard. I prayed hard. I had slip ups and setbacks. But I prayed, I asked for strength, and I persevered.

If you had asked me back when I first got to prison if I could ever forgive my mother, I would have laughed at the idea. But, eventually, that's exactly what I did. I made peace with my mother. I came to forgive her. I realized that she was a broken woman. She was an alcoholic, she had been abused and like so many people, she didn't know how to deal with problems. Like most of the things in my life, learning to overcome the anger I had held toward my mother for so long wasn't easy. But I did.

Years later, I received word at the prison that my mother was dying in the hospital. I was given a choice: I could go for one final visit, or I could go to the funeral, but I couldn't do both. I remember thinking it was a tough decision at the time. There would be a lot of people at the funeral, people I had not seen for many years. It was tempting. But in the end, I chose to see my mother while she was still alive. I was shackled with a thick chain around my waist and chains connecting my handcuffs to my waist and my ankles to my waist. They cleared the hall my mother's room was in and I was escorted by two armed officers to her room. By the time I got to her, she was basically gone. A machine was keeping her alive, but I'm sure she knew I was there. I told her I loved her and would miss her. I knew that just like the nuns had told me, I had to forgive those around me and I had to forgive myself. I think this visit served dual purposes. I was there to make my final peace with the woman who had caused me so much pain and suffering. But it was going to end that day. I had come to grips with my mother years earlier, but this was to be a total, final cleansing of the slate.

But equally important, I was on a mission to forgive myself. If you have explored psychology or done much in the way of soul-searching, you know that at times it can be easier to forgive your worst enemy than to forgive yourself. Something told me that had I not gone to say goodbye to my mother one last time, it would simply add to the things in my life that I would be forced to reconcile on my long, dark journey of self-forgiveness.

****

I am also writing this book and devoting whatever days I have left on Earth to spreading a message of the harsh realities that come with trying to live a thug life for another reason. I do it for Ashley. Ashley is a young woman who heard me speak at one of my high school presentations. When I got home that night and checked in on Facebook, I found the following note:

I'm not gonna lie ... when you started talking about your story and said that you were in prison for killing I was scared outta my mind, But once you started telling your story I really got interested and it made me realize what will happen if I stay on the path I am on right now. So again I thank you for coming in and speaking to us. –Ashley

I've spoken to thousands of young people like Ashley since I was released from prison. They have varying degrees of the same tragic story. They are good kids making bad choices. Hanging with the wrong crowd, getting mixed up with drugs, cutting class, drinking, stealing, carrying weapons, you name it, and these kids are doing it. One thing that always amazes me is that these kids will hear me speak for 45 minutes and be ready to pour their hearts out to me. They don't want to talk about their problems with their parents, teachers or clergy because they don't want to be judged or punished. They want to be valued and they want to be helped. Anyone who meets me quickly discovers one thing: I am in no position to judge anyone. So I listen and I offer them advice and support. I don't condone their bad behavior; in fact, I am brutally blunt about what will happen to them if they keep up the life some of them are living. But I never judge them and I never treat them like they are just a kid. I treat everyone as my equal, and the kids respond.

At the end of most of my presentations, I usually put my Facebook address and email up on the screen for the students. Then I invite them to say hello and grab a business card on the way out the door. It's during those times that I hear some of the most gut-wrenching stories you'll ever think of. The number of young people filled with pain, who are suffering, who are trying to dull their pain with drugs and alcohol or who are contemplating suicide is shocking.

What makes it worse is that the government seems to think the answer is to build more prisons. Prison is a big business in this country and anybody who thinks locking someone up has anything to do with rehabilitating them is naïve. Prisons are a revolving door system because the people in charge want them to be. They need prisoners in order to keep their jobs, plain and simple. So instead of trying to do more to reach these kids when they are young, they just herd them down a path that is leading more and more of them into the prison system.

That's why I am working so hard to reach these kids. And I'm not alone. There are others out there trying to get through to a generation of youth that seem increasingly lost. But we are fighting an uphill battle because the system is set up to make these kids fail and when they fail, the people who work in prisons, rehabs, and the "misery industry" of many human and Social Service profit. During my time working in the drug and alcohol rehab, it was a joke. I saw the same people come in over and over. They would get released when the allotted time was up, but we all knew they would be back as soon as they were eligible. It's the way the system works. I believe the key is to reach these young people as early as possible. And I don't come to them with some sugar-coated "Just Say No" message because it doesn't work. You come in telling them how drugs will kill them, and they tune you out. But when I come in and tell them what it is like to worry every day if another man is going to rape you in the shower, it gets their attention. When I talk about having to eat turkey out of my toilet bowl because it was the only way to keep it cold, they listen. When I tell them the reality – not the television stuff they see, but the cold, harsh reality of life in prison – they listen. I may not reach every one of them, but I don't plan to quit until I have made the best effort I can.

The politicians ignore the problem, the teachers are too overworked to deal with it, the parents are too busy to pay attention and see what is right under their noses, and so more and more young people are spiraling out of control.

So when people ask me, 'Jerry, why do you bother? You spent more than half your life in prison, why not just kick back and enjoy yourself?' the answer is simple. This is my calling. It is why I beat those insurmountable odds and earned my parole. It wasn't to sit back and watch television. It wasn't to try and catch up on everything I missed out on in my life. It was to save lives. I never had kids of my own, but I feel like in a way every kid I reach with my message is a chance to impart some wisdom, share some guidance and direction and make a difference in their lives.

So, no matter how much I personally struggle, I will continue to speak out. Some people may not like it, but that won't stop me. The message is too important to give up. Lives hang in the balance, and I will continue to fight for every person I meet until I take my last breath.

Chapter 16

After Christine and I divorced, nothing really changed for me. As much as she had worked with me to write letters and campaign for my release, it hadn't worked. Besides, I had spent a lifetime going it alone, so in the big picture, the few years I spent with her were a blip on the radar.

With her gone, I just kept grinding. I continued to take every class I could, kept writing letters to anyone who might listen and continued to work as a leader in the prison, and helping other prisoners with everything from education, to preparing for their own parole hearings, to fitness and nutrition advice.

I knew what I was up against. I was only one amongst over 60,000 prisoners in the system in this state. I made a promise to myself that I would not be just another brick in the wall. I knew that if I was ever going to convince a parole board to release me, I had to think like they thought. I studied everything I could on the criminal personality. I more or less read all of the same books they read. I learned that if I was going to get out, I had to take full responsibility for what I had done, show how remorseful I was, convince them of my rehabilitation thought all of the academic and therapeutic programs I had taken, and have excellent release plans. I became teachable and was always questioning everyone about everything. I had to get rid of all of my pre-conceived notions about many things.

I started thinking and acting like a parole commissioner. I started doing mock interviews with men attending parole hearings and I would look at their pre-sentence reports, criminal history rap sheets, sentencing minutes, disciplinary reports, proof of rehabilitation, etc. I would call myself, "Commissioner Hardass," and I would ask all of the questions I knew would be asked of the men appearing in front of a parole board. Most of the men had no idea what to say or do upon entering the hearing room but once we got through preparing together, they knew what to expect and how to respond.

I've tried to sprinkle some guidance and advice into this book, and here is another thing I want you to walk away with: I never gave up. You've all heard the clichés: Winners never quit and quitters never win. It sounds good on a poster, but most people read positive affirmations or inspirational quotes and they smile, maybe they think about it during that day, but then they forget about it. What I am telling you isn't some feel-good quote. It is the reality I took from spending 37 years of my life locked in a cage, treated like I was less than an animal. So when I tell you not to ever quit, not to ever give up, I'm not telling you to do anything I didn't do in my own life. Every time I was turned away for parole, it would have been easy to quit. Instead, I just worked harder. Every person who told me I would never be released, just made me more driven, more determined to prove them wrong.

At one point, back in 1999 I was a prisoner in Ossining Correctional Facility – Sing Sing. Someone turned rat and said that a bunch of prisoners were planning a protest against prison conditions. I was fingered as one of the ring leaders. It wasn't true, but in prison, some guys will say whatever it takes to get a better deal for themselves. By this point in my sentence I had become an activist for better prison conditions and was using my education. I fought for what was right, and rubbed the administration the wrong way. Do I think they went after me and used a mysterious "confidential informant" to pin a bogus charge on me? Well … I will say this much: I was never a leader in any planned protest, but that didn't matter to them. I was shipped out to Upstate Correctional Facility and ordered to spend 18 months in solitary confinement, or as we called it, "The Box."

If existing in a maximum security prison is hell on Earth, living in "The Box" is something buried so far beneath hell that you aspire to return to hell.

They wanted me out of Sing Sing and this was the way it was done. Except they underestimated one thing: I never give up. I had no money to hire an attorney. I had no real voice or influence, all I had was my body, and so I used the only thing I owned to shine a light on the injustice that had occurred. I announced that I was going on a hunger strike. I refused all food and drank just three small cups of water each day. I wanted people to hear about what was going on inside the walls of the prison. We were prisoners and many of us deserved to be where we were, but we still had rights. We still deserved to be treated with basic care and protections afforded us under the United States Constitution.

Lots of guys will say they are doing a hunger strike in prison, so in that regard, I wasn't unique. The thing is, they last a day or two, then they get hungry and they crack. Or, the guards get to them. The prisons don't want any attention from the outside world, so things like prisoners refusing food is bad for business. But I wasn't like most prisoners. I never gave up. As the days wore on and I continued to refuse food, they sent chaplains to talk with me. They sent prison officials; they had other prisoners trying to get me to eat. But I held my ground. Christine was my advocate in the free world. This was a protest, and I wasn't giving in until my voice was heard. Once I got a few weeks into my strike, the media picked up on the story. The *Times Union Newspaper* sent a reporter to visit me and wrote an in-depth piece on my plight. I told him at the time, I planned to go 40 days and nights without food. It was Biblical for me and I wasn't giving up. And I didn't. I drew the parallel of David and Goliath and it wasn't just a sound bite. I really saw my mission as bigger than just Jerry Balone getting out of solitary. I saw this as a chance to slay the beast, to take a stand for every other guy locked down with me. I had a chance to create real reform and if it took some personal sacrifice and some physical pain, then it was well worth it. For someone who had spent his entire life living an incredibly selfish existence, this was a different way of looking at the world. Sure, I wanted out of the Box, but I also wanted to make people aware, to be an activist, to lend my voice, or in this case my body, to those around me. The hunger strike was a turning point in my life. Not only did I make it the full 40 days, but within a few months, I won a complete reversal of the charges and was transferred to Elmira.

So when I tell young people not to give up, not to quit, they aren't just hollow words. I tell them, wake up tomorrow and don't eat a thing all day. Tell me what you feel like when it is time for bed. If you make it all day, and most of you couldn't, then imagine doing it for 39 more days. Then imagine doing it without anything to distract you from the painful hunger pains. No computer, no iPod, no trips to the mall, nothing. I spent 40 days in a cage and refused food because I was determined. I did it because I knew it was my only card to play. And most importantly, I did it because I was innocent.

****

Despite my iron-clad resolve to keep fighting for my freedom, nobody seemed to be listening. I was a changed man, so far removed from that angry, violent thug who committed those murders back in 1973 that he was unrecognizable to me. But within the system, no one could get past what they called, "the nature of my crime."

In 2003, when I was turned down for parole for the fifth time, my parole decision read like every one of them before it.

Discretionary release is inappropriate based upon the heinous nature of the instant offense which clearly illustrates the depraved indifference to human life you have demonstrated.

I've always said these parole hearings are rubber-stamped and the proof is the fact that every two years they would just write the exact same things in the denial. Despite earning hundreds of letters of commendation, certificates, degrees and awards, none of that mattered. Two years later I returned to the parole board and again, parole was denied.

This panel finds your release is incompatible with the public safety and welfare. Due to the violence of the instant offenses and clear intent to subject others to harm shown by obtaining, carrying and ultimately using a hand gun, your release at this time is denied.

The verbiage may have changed a bit, but it always came back to the nature of my crime. I, of course, was walking a fine line. To be considered for parole, you must accept full responsibility for the crimes that you committed. I had to accept full responsibility for the deaths of my three victims even though there were two of us who were convicted of participating in this horrible crime. Anything less would be seen as lacking remorse and I would be denied. So I had to accept responsibility for part of the crime I didn't commit. I also had to be very careful when pleading my case. As proud as I was of all that I had accomplished in prison, it didn't bring back those three people to their families. If I came across as too indignant for my own plight, that would sour the parole board. It was a chess game, and one that I intended to win, but like all games of skill, I had to be methodical and strategic in how I approached "the game".

Part of me loved the challenge. It allowed me to use my education, to research, to investigate, to be relentless in my pursuit of freedom. It kept me busy and it staved off the boredom that is so excruciating on the inside.

But another part of me saw it for what it was –a fruitless attempt to beat a system that was set up for every single prisoner to fail. If the parole system was unfair, and I absolutely knew that it was, then what did anything else even matter? I knew they were making their decisions without even considering my interview, or my academic and therapeutic accomplishments. The system was rigged, and after being denied parole in 2005, my sixth denial since I became eligible in 1995, I knew I was going to die in prison unless I took drastic measures. I had two years until I was eligible for parole again, and for me, that meant two years to turn the heat up on the State, to expose the system for what it was, and to force their hand and earn my release. I knew it was a fight that would make my hunger strike seem like skipping a single meal. It was a fight that would take an inner-strength that even I wasn't sure I had. But I knew that after six denials of parole, my window of opportunity, which was paper-thin to begin with, was closing fast. It was now or never, and I intended to make it now.

****

I spent years in a letter-writing campaign to expose the parole system as a broken shell of what it was intended to be. I woke every morning in my cell or cube and mapped out who I was going to write to that day. I wrote letters seven days a week. I wrote to prison officials. I sent Freedom of Information Law FOIL requests for every decision that had ever been handed down in my case. I demanded notes, memos, and internal correspondence. I was determined to find enough to prove what

I knew to be true. Meanwhile, I wrote to local politicians. I wrote to New York Governor George Pataki. I wrote to Governor Eliot Spitzer. I wrote to my United States Senator Charles Schumer and other politicians. I wrote to the leaders of the Catholic Church and other faiths. I wrote to the media. Most people ignored me, others sent form letters or in some cases, caustic replies. But some listened. I was never deterred. Eventually, people began to question the system and wonder if prisoner No. 74C-0264 might be onto something.

Still, I knew pressure from the outside wouldn't be enough. I had to convince the prison and parole officials that I was never going to quit working towards my freedom. For lack of a better word, I figured my best plan was to be the biggest pain in the system I could be, until they decided it would be easier to set me free and shut me up, then to deny me and face the wrath of my unending publicity campaign.

Anytime you decide to buck the system, you run the risk of it getting messy. I knew I was going after the very people who controlled my every move. I knew I ran the risk of getting transferred to the worst prison they could find. There were all kinds of internal screws they could twist to make my time as difficult as possible. At least that's what they thought. I knew that every day I was locked up was rock-bottom for me, and nothing they could do could make it any worse. So I pushed ahead, and waged an all-out assault on the New York State Division of Parole. If this was war, then I was making a tactically crazy move, but it was a move that would eventually pay the ultimate dividend.

Chapter 17

Every day I wake up as a free man is a blessing. But I would be lying if I said things were going entirely well for me. In an economy with near 10 percent of the people unemployed, living in the poorest section of the third poorest city in America, opportunities are few and far between. And, that's if you are a man without baggage. Paint a "convicted murderer" scarlet letter across your resume and opportunities become virtually non-existent.

In prison I earned $3.00 a week. Unless you had someone in the free world sending you money and packages every month, you either had to do without or learn some type of hustle. Most of the things people do in prison to survive are illegal: gambling, drug selling, making and drinking homemade wine, extortion, stealing food out of the mess hall, etc.

Some people become artists, writers, experts at law, personal fitness trainers. At one time, prisoners were allowed to do all sorts of arts and crafts in their cells. Things like making glass paintings, leather work where you could make belts or purses for family members, etc. All of this was eventually taken away because of so-called security issues. There were many prisoners who when released had thousands of dollars to start out a new life. I had a little over $150.00 when I cashed my check upon my release. If anyone was ever set up for failure, it was me.

Though I love what I do speaking in the schools and churches, most of the time there is no money involved. Not that I am looking to get rich in my life. When you have spent most of your existence subsiding on nothing, it doesn't take much to satisfy you. But like anyone else, I wanted to be able to afford nice clothes, to be able to go out to dinner at places other than McDonalds, Subways or eating chicken wings and pizza all the time. I want to have a modest sense of security. I will never accumulate enough points to obtain social security benefits when I turn 65. I more or less will have to work until the day I die.

But the truth is, if I live the rest of my life in poverty, if I die penniless, if I live out my days struggling to the end, I'm OK with that. We all have our crosses to bear, and if this is mine, so be it. Money comes and goes, but the success I really want is the kind that will allow me to continue to share my story and spread my message of hope. That's what this book is about. It's a vehicle for me to reach people who are hurting. Families that are broken, kids who are where I was, people who are watching their loved one slip away right before their eyes. People in prison who believe that rehabilitation and redemption are not possible because of what they did that sent them to prison. I want this book to open doors for more opportunities to speak. Since my release, I have appeared on television and radio worldwide. My story appeared on the 700 Club and I have spoken to over 300 audiences in and around the Buffalo, NY area. Many stories have been written about the work that I'm doing. I see this book as one tool in my chest. One weapon to offer hope and the possibility of a brighter future to each person that picks it up. But I also see it as opening doors to bigger audiences. There are literally millions of lost children living in this country. You know some of them. They are your sons and daughters. They are your neighbors, your nieces, and your co-worker's children. I want to meet and touch them all. Every one of them. Sound crazy? Good. Because if you ask me, one of the reasons we are having the problems we are, not only with our youth, but with the country as a whole, is because too few are willing to reach outside of themselves to make a difference. We want to give, but not 'till it hurts. We want to help out, but only when it is convenient for our schedules. We want to reach a few but there is only so much one person can do, right?

Wrong. I believe we can stretch ourselves, push the boundaries and change the world right here where each of us stands. It's what I intend to do and since you are reading this book, I hope it is something you will consider doing. Each of us has an incredible story to tell and valuable insight we can pass along to the next generation. You may not have my story, but then again, I don't have yours. Together, we can all add to the tapestry and weave a collective life worth sharing with the world. I don't know most of you, though I hope I get to meet each one of you someday. But I do know that you have gifts and talents to offer.

There are young people around you every day who need more people they can look up to. It isn't about how much money you make, or what kind of car you drive. It's about living your life with integrity and being someone they hope to become like and respect. If a career criminal who spent almost four decades in prison for murder can connect with these kids, then you really don't have an excuse.

What you do have is a chance to change lives. A chance to reach the lost and make a difference that is beyond anything in your wildest dreams. Don't finish this book and put it up on a shelf and make it another interesting book you've read. If you don't turn the last page and come away feeling compelled to make a difference, I've failed.

Maybe young people aren't your calling. That's OK. Because there are hundreds of thousands of prisoners locked up in this country that are in desperate need of hope, of someone who believes in them. In most of the prisons I lived in, there might be 1,000 prisoners at any given time. Out of those, maybe three dozen of them ever got visits that weren't from a lawyer. For much of the prison population in this country, when the cell door closes behind them, they are dead to the outside world. Friends fall away, relatives shun them, and significant others move on. It is an incredibly lonely life, and contrary to what you may often hear in popular media, there are a lot of good people in prison.

There are also countless programs where you can write to prisoners, send care packages or even volunteer in the prison, if you have one near where you live. So whatever you do, do something. Step beyond your own comfortable world and seize the opportunity to make a difference. Like I told you before, I only preach what I practice. I hate prisons, as you might imagine. When I walked away from Fishkill in 2007, I swore I would never set foot inside a prison again. But God had a different plan for my life. Now, I visit the Orleans Correctional Facility every three months to speak with prisoners who are getting ready to be released. I hate it every time I pull up to the gates of the prison, but I also know how much encouragement and inspiration meant to me when I was locked up, and so I go and serve. When I speak to kids, my goal is to keep them from going to prison. When I speak at Orleans, my goal is to keep the prisoners from going *back* to prison once they are released. I work hard to show the kids how tough life is on the inside and I work with these guys to show them how tough life is going to be on the *outside.*

I was blindsided when I left prison and I make sure they understand that. Many of the prison re-entry programs on the whole do a really poor job of preparing prisoners for a return to society. I tell it how it is. No one cares that I have five college degrees. No one cares that I am a hard worker. No one cares that I am proficient in many different skilled areas. They see me as a criminal and killer, end of story. As I look around the room at Orleans, I know most of these guys will be back within a year. They will come out expecting to land a job, a girl, a place to live, and ease back into life. What they don't know, is when you get locked up, your world leaves you behind. There are no jobs waiting for you, no made-for-television crowds waiting with balloons when you walk out those gates. No one cares what you did to get locked up and no one cares how much you accomplished on the inside. To most people, your life is boiled down to one word: felon. It's the reality that I try to get across to the men at Orleans. Most of what they hear is all the rosy side of getting out. The truth is, it is tough to make it out here. It is a dogfight every day. The only person looking out for me is me. Each day I walk out my front door, there are a thousand-and-one ways I could violate my parole and the board would be only too happy to send me back to prison to die. But, much like with the young people, I try to serve as an inspiration to the prisoners. A sort of, "If I can do it, anybody can do it," story. I tell them how my worst day outside is better than my best day in prison. I let them know how hard the struggle is going to be. I tell them that many of them are coming back because they won't cut it on the outside. They scoff, shake their heads, and curse me under their breath. But I'm right. The statics bear it out. And worse yet, I've been speaking at Orleans long enough that I am seeing the same faces recycled through. They were released, reoffended, returned to prison, and now, are preparing to be released a second and third time. Prison is like a high-speed train, once you get on, it can be tough to get off.

Most men getting out of prison suffer from some form of Post Traumatic Stress Disorder (PTSD). Especially if they served most of their time in maximum security prisons. I can honestly say that I witnessed thousands of acts of violence during my long incarceration. Every time you step out of your cell, there is a good chance that some type of violence may take place. When we come back to the "free world," it takes time to adjust. We're no different than those coming back from a war except that we lived it 24 hours a day for five, ten, fifteen or more years with no breaks in between. I believe this is one of the major reasons that those of us who were incarcerated for long periods of time cannot maintain meaningful relationships.

About the best advice I can give to anyone in prison is that when they get out, they need to think about going into business for themselves. I've tried every get rich scheme there is on the internet. I always say that I would trade in my two master's degrees for a carpentry or welding certificate. I now work for myself doing snow plowing and landscaping work or anything else I can find. I didn't know how to do much of anything when I got out but I've become pretty good at what I do and have met a lot of interesting people along the way. One thing that has helped me out tremendously is that I have never been late for one appointment, work assignment or anything else. Like prison, I know where I have to be and I'm always there.

The reaction I get from the prisoners is similar to what I get from some of the students I speak to. When I visit kids in a suburban setting, many of them scoff at me and slouch in their chairs. Just like the ghetto kids, you can practically hear them saying under their breath. I'll never end up there. But the truth is, with the boom in the drug trade, they are exactly the kids who end up doing a two-year stretch in Attica. These prep school kids who have lived such a sheltered life get caught dealing a few bags of crack and then next thing they know, they are locked up to become somebody's "girlfriend" on the inside: and their life is changed forever.

On the other end of the spectrum are the inner-city kids. I speak at Niagara Falls High School every year, and despite the beauty of the Falls, the city is a tough place and the students in the high school are as tough as they come. At least they think they are.

As you look out over the auditorium, this is a group that largely sees themselves as cooler than some washed up old convict lecturing them. The group is typically split in half: The ones who don't think they will ever end up in prison, and the group that sees themselves as hard-core thugs who practically want to go to prison.

This is where popular culture comes into play and really screws these kids over. Life in prison isn't what they show you in the movies and it isn't what the rap music makes it out to be. When Tupac Shakur got sent upstate in 1994, he spent a few years in Clinton Correctional Facility. When he came out, he talked about how he wrote great music while he was in prison and he drew from the experience. He glorified it in his subsequent music and videos. A generation of disenfranchised youth bought into it and saw prison "Thug Life" as an escape from their lives on the outside. There is just one small problem. At the time of his incarceration, Shakur had already sold millions of albums and was a worldwide celebrity. Do you think he got the same treatment in prison as Jerry Balone did, or as you would? Hell no. He was a celebrity on the outside and he was a celebrity on the inside. He got treated with kid gloves and did the softest time imaginable. Guys like that do more damage to young people than anyone. He gets the soft sentence, and then sells albums on the back of prison life, portraying it as part of some slick rite of passage for young people.

I tell this to my audience, but they are without a doubt, the toughest nut to crack. I ask these students how many of them know someone currently locked up in prison. When I ask that question in a suburb, I might get one or two hands, often none. When I pose the same question in Niagara Falls, hands shoot up all across the room. Later, as we talk after the presentation, I will hear stories of fathers, mothers, brothers, and uncles all incarcerated many of them for drug-related offenses. You would think that seeing first-hand the pain and destruction the lifestyle causes, these kids would run as fast as they could in the opposite direction. But they don't. Instead, they see their life as inevitable. It's as though the script has already been written and they are just actors playing the part. It breaks my heart to see it, but the reality is, I know many of these kids, some as young as 15-years-old, will be in prison by the time they are 18, following in the darkened footsteps of their ill-fated family members. The cycle will continue until someone finds the strength to break it. And that is the true tragedy.

Chapter 18

It was the spring of 2007 and I was heading full steam ahead for my seventh parole board. April marked 33 years I had been in prison (not counting the time I spent in Elmira, Coxsackie and Comstock for the robbery conviction prior to the murders). I had spent more than 12,000 days and night behind bars for the crimes I committed. Though I don't spend time dwelling on what might have been, as I write this now, as I type that number into the computer, it gives me pause to wonder. What if they had gone to Florida? What if we scrapped the plan to rob the house? What if we had left the guns at home? So many things, small things, nuances, could have changed the entire outcome of my life.

The truth is, if I hadn't gone to prison for that particular crime, it would have been for something else. It was only a matter of time. I didn't have the ability to live among people in a civilized society. In a strange way, I needed prison. I wish it wasn't that way, but that's the reality. Without any parental figures, without a strong support network in school, I had nothing and no one to guide me. I had no one willing or able to get me back on track, and I didn't care enough about anyone around me, much less myself, enough to make any changes. I was self-destructive from as young as I can remember, and in reality, prison probably saved my life.

But here I was 12,000 days later. I was a 55-year-old man. I had never held a steady job, never had children, and never paid taxes. I had no friends, no relatives that stayed in contact with me; I was a career criminal who most people had written off decades ago. But I hadn't. There was a reason I had survived so long in prison. There was a reason I had been transferred to Shawangunk and had the chance to take the education classes. There was a reason the Dominican Nuns had decided to write to me when there were thousands of other prisoners they could have reached out to. There was a reason that people from all over the country were willing to write letters supporting my release. I had a destiny. I believed that then and I believe it now.

You have a destiny, too. Maybe you are already fulfilling yours, or maybe you don't believe you have any greater purpose, but you do. I'm living proof that God has a plan for all of us, and each and every time I had a setback in prison, I knew it was just making me stronger for the day when I would be set free to begin fulfilling that plan for my life.

My parole hearing was set for June of 2007. I had worked harder than ever on my two-pronged approach to gaining my freedom. On the positive side, I continued to avail myself of every therapeutic program and prisoner assistance program the prison system offered. But, I often doubted that would ever be enough to earn my release in the eyes of the parole parole board. So I had spent the final two years of my incarceration putting more heat on the prison system to release my records, to investigate the parole commissioners, to conduct an internal investigation of their own system. I was involved in a federal class action lawsuit against the parole board.

I knew if I could get people to start turning over some rocks, they would see what lived underneath. But, I also knew that the last thing the State wanted was any kind of investigation. If I could prove that the parole board was acting in violation of my rights, then it would call into question their decision on every prisoner that had ever come before them. Tens of thousands of cases would have to be reopened, the cost would be astronomical and the public black eye it would give the system would be too much for it to bear.

Such a review also posed the real possibility that hundreds, if not thousands of prisoners could win release if it was found that their hearings were conducted unjustly. In my mind, I figured they would rather let me go and shut me up, than risk having to turn thousands of prisoners free. Remember: keeping people locked up is a business. It is the livelihood of thousands of corrections and other related-service employees. I was acutely aware that everyone from the guards, to the wardens, to the prison commissioner - would go to great lengths to protect that livelihood.

My hearing came and went, and on the surface, it was just like all of the others. I submitted my portfolio, sat down for an interview, and then went back to my block to wait for a decision. Though I had learned not to get my hopes up, I knew this one had the chance to be different. My stellar educational achievement, dedicated therapeutic work, clean record, and awaiting support system just might, I thought, be sufficient justification to let me go without looking bad in the public eye.

That's what it comes down to half the time: public relations. The board knew there would be a lot of heat on them for allowing parole to a triple-murderer. I'm guessing the way they saw it was this: They assumed I would come out, commit a crime fairly quickly, and get my ticket punched to come right back and die in my cell. The hope of course, would be that I did a robbery or some relatively petty crime. If I came out and murdered someone, well, that would really be sticky for them to explain. But even then, they would point to the letters of commendation, the positive evaluations, the political support for my release, and they would pass the buck. Either way, I was trying to obtain a win-win situation where they could hold me up to other prisoners and say that if they did the right thing, they, too, could one day earn parole.

I'll never forget the day my decision came. You could tell the answer before you even opened the envelope. A denial always came in a thick envelope with an appeal form. After all, there wasn't much to say: Denied, see you again in two years. When people earned parole, the envelope was thin. There were explanations of what would happen, how the process would go and when you would be released.

At Fishkill, guys were called down to the desk for mail. Everyone in prison knows when a parole board meets and when the decisions come to the block. A sergeant was responsible for delivering the results to each dorm officer and he had to personally hand it to you after he checked your identification. My decision was given to me three days after my hearing. One of the guys in my dorm informed me that the sergeant had delivered the parole decisions and that mine was in a thin envelope. He said he had actually felt it. My heart began to beat fast. Could this be the one? The anticipation was killing me.

Finally, I got the call. I headed down to the desk to pick up my mail. By now, the buzz had made its way around the block that I had a thin envelope and when I picked up my mail, there were about 30 other prisoners and a buzz surrounding me.

Come on Jerry, open it up. Let's see it. My hands were trembling. I held the envelope and examined it. It did feel thinner than the six previous ones I had received. I had known guys who received thin envelopes and were given two years but the parole department forgot to put an appeal form in it. You can be sure this crossed my mind as I was standing there. I held my breath. Everyone wanted to touch the envelope and hold it up to the light to see what was inside of it. *Let's go Jerry, open it before we open it for you,* one guy yelled. I knew the odds were long, but I was praying for my Golden Ticket. I ripped it open and unfolded the paper inside. A smile broke out across my face and the cell block erupted in raucous screams and shouts. I was going home.

****

The coming days and weeks were a blur. Word got around the prison that Jerry was going home. Prison is usually such a negative, angry place; so the announcement of my parole was like a breath of fresh air into a place that desperately needed it. Suddenly, guys who had long ago given up hope of ever being free again, now had hope. Guys figured, Well, if Jerry got out, then why not me? Everybody wanted a piece of me. They wanted to pick my brain, to get me to help them. What did I do? How did I beat the system?

Guys who had parole hearings coming up began to expect their release. Mind you, these were prisoners that had never prepared for their hearings, never made any effort to improve their chances of parole. Now suddenly, they expected to be released because in their minds, their crimes were not as bad as mine. Now, if they let the murderer free, it was somehow supposed to open the gates and be parole for everyone. The truth was, I had devoted tens of thousands of hours to earning my release. I spent approximately 18 years day in and day out preparing for it. While guys were playing cards or shooting dice, I was writing letters. While they were sleeping, watching television or playing basketball in the yard, I was researching case law. While they were running their game in the prison, I was working with deliberation to plan for my life on the outside.

I labored and struggled to earn my release, and - as my fellow prisoners soon found out - letting me go wasn't a signal that there was a shift in the approach of the parole board. There was not going to be a mass release. In fact, many of the men who I did time with are still locked up, still waiting for that thin letter to come in the mail. Unfortunately, for many of them, they are destined to spend the rest of their days counting down their life in two-year increments, waiting for their next parole hearing and a letter that will never come.

One of the first things I did upon my release was write a book about my experiences with the parole board because everyone kept telling me how lucky I was. My book, *A Former Prisoner's Guide to Parole*, is a step-by-step history of the process I followed to obtain my release. It is a book that should be given to every prisoner upon entering the system to help them avoid many of the mistakes I made early in my sentence. Many have read it and followed my advice and are now out here in the free world enjoying all that life has to offer.

As part of my parole, I can't associate with convicted felons, so I can't have any direct contact with Tommy and many of my other friends who are still on the inside. There are many reasons why I want to win my freedom from parole. One of them is so I can reach out to Tommy. I would like to be able to send him some care packages, to make sure he has money in his commissary. It might sound crazy, but in my life, he was, and still is, family. He and I will forever be linked by what we did. I will always have a connection with him and I want to do whatever I can to help him out. I also live with guilt that I am unable to send money and packages to him and the friends I left behind on the inside.

The bottom line is that every dime I make right now goes for bills. Almost every piece of furniture in my home is second hand. I have an association with many of the people who work in thrift stores in the Buffalo, NY area. I never imagined being out here wearing someone's second hand clothes, but at least they look, fit, and feel better than the prison uniforms I was forced to wear on the inside.

It's a part of prison life that people on the outside can never fully understand. Although you never really know who you can trust and who your friends are in prison, you do get close to people. You develop bonds. In a place where most of us had no family, no friends, no money, no possessions, we had each other. It's sort of like the prison code you've heard about. If a guy gets convicted of abusing a child, he is in for a rough time in prison. There is a hierarchy among guys on the inside. We created our own laws, our own rules, and we became, to some degree, our own family.

So if Tommy called me up, or one of the other guys wrote to me and needed something, if I was off parole, I would do what I could. It's a code, sort of "honor among thieves," and when you spend more than half your life inside a cage, you don't just get rid of that subculture with a hot shower on the outside.

Chapter 19

There is a funny thing about being free: It comes with a price. I know I'm a marked man forever. It has been almost five years since my release, and yet every morning when I leave my house, I do so with the assumption that it could be the last time I see it again. Under the terms of my parole I have nothing that is my own. They can listen to my phone calls, read my emails, follow me, and search my car, my home, and my person. I will live the rest of my life under a cloud of suspicion. I am a convicted felon. I am a thief and a murderer, and those labels will stick with me long after I leave this Earth. For better or for worse, they are my legacy. All I can hope to do is keep striving as making it for the better.

My life today is in many ways, similar to what it was during my last years in prison. I live in fear, act with trepidation. I answer to the authorities and am free at their will. Back then, I shared a message of hope with convicts. Now, I share the message with students. Back then, I planned and dreamed of my future. Today, I do the same thing. On the inside, I was living in those two-year stretches, waiting for a letter saying I was free. Today, I am living my life in two-year stretches, waiting for my parole officer to deem me no longer necessary to be monitored like a child.

I don't know that I will ever be released from parole, and if I am not, that's OK. I'll continue to do what I can do. I will continue to fight for myself, fight for the children of our community and fight to work on behalf of the prisoners I left behind when I walked free into the light and fresh air of 2007.

To that last point, prisoner's rights and advocating for both those who remain locked up, as well as those who are being released back into society and are virtually doomed for failure has become a mission for me: I am called to fight for those with no voice.

Our legal system in this country is broken. Our prison system in this country is broken. Our system for paroling people out of prison with no education or vocational skills is broken. Yet because those it affects are primarily the disenfranchised members of our society, very little is done to fix any of it. Sure, there are advocacy groups out there fighting for prisoner's rights, and some of them do wonderful work. But like far too much in this country, there is often rampant corruption even in the reform circles. Many of these programs receive tens of thousands of dollars in funding from the federal and state government to assist with, for example, prisoner re-entry programs.

These are programs similar to what I was in at Cephas where individuals who are being released are assisted with the transition back into society. The program at Cephas has statistics to prove that prove that it works – many others do not. Despite the funding, many other re-entry programs do very little to offer former prisoners meaningful transition. Instead, they accept donations and pass out used clothing and used furniture, require you to sign up for every form of government assistance there is, so that in the end, what do they truly offer to the formerly incarcerated and for the benefit of the community? Quite often, the answer is not too much.

Where does the rest of the money go? Well, much of it gets eaten up in "administrative costs," meaning, it doesn't go for the people it is intended to serve. While there may have been good intentions behind the formation of many of these programs, and some of them do indeed do some good, too many of them are cash cows for a few and offer little in the way of meaningful re-entry assistance to those they are paid to assist.

But don't take my word for it. The numbers don't lie. According to a 2011 study, the national rate of recidivism in the United States is more than 67 percent. More than two out of three adults who leave prison return within three years. How can we say a system is working when it fails two out of every three people it is paid to serve? Now obviously, some of the responsibility lies with the ex-convict. I'm certainly not putting all of the blame on the system. But what I am saying is that our system is set up for failure.

For the sake of this discussion, I won't even go into the racial inequality in the legal system, although it is a dominant problem as evidenced by the percentage of minorities in the prison system and the unjust disproportionate sentences they often receive. But to keep it simple, let's take a person convicted of a felony in the United States today. While you might think a felony means rape, murder and armed robbery, felonies can include Driving Under the Influence (DUI), white collar crimes like theft of money and even a relatively innocuous crime like writing a bad check. While every crime deserves a just punishment, let's look at what happens if you are convicted of aggravated DUI, a felony. You hire a lawyer, reach a plea, serve a jail sentence, pay your fines and earn your release. By now, you have lost your job, your name has appeared in the newspaper, and you have paid a steep price for your crime. Now, in theory, upon release, the state has deemed you to have paid your debt to society and releases you. But your life is far from normal. You may have paid your debt, but you are now labeled a felon. Try to find a job application that doesn't ask if you have been convicted of a felony. Then check yes, and see how many call backs you get.

Now you are in a position where no one will hire you. But at least you have a place to live, right? Not so fast. More and more landlords are conducting background checks when renting an apartment. So before you know it, you have no place to live and no job to support yourself. But you paid your debt to society didn't you? Seems like that isn't enough in our system. So now, with no job and thus no money, what do you do? You turn to what you know best – or picked up in the system while serving out that DUI conviction. Or, if you went in for dealing drugs, you go back to drugs. Gambling, robbery, whatever sent you away is what you turn to when you are out of options. Now you can see how two thirds of ex-convicts end up back behind bars.

Take away a man's (or woman's) ability to earn a living and have a roof over their head, and what do you expect to happen? The permanent labeling of non-violent offenders with the felony tag is crippling to their rehabilitation and in the end, costs the taxpayers when they are returned to prison. But remember what

I said, prison is big business, and those at the top love to keep the system's rewards for themselves. If you owned an apartment complex, and people kept moving out of your rental units and you couldn't fill their spots, you would go bankrupt. Prison is no different. The system is built to fill every cell, and usually over fill them. Empty cells equal lost revenue for the government, and if there is one thing the government hates, it is losing out on the chance to line its collective coffers with cash.

So I advocate. I travel wherever I am invited. I take the message to the radio, I take it to television. I advocate through social media. I work with re-entry programs to make a greater, more genuine difference. I was able to convince the reporter from The Buffalo Law Journal that I was sincere in my efforts to assist in keeping young people out of the criminal justice system or embarking on a lifetime addiction to drugs and alcohol. In some circles, I am seen as an expert, having been there and done that, and my voice is heard. In other circles, I am seen as a murderer and a felon and dismissed as such. No matter, I will continue this fight until we see more measured equality in the administration of justice in this country. I may be one of the lucky ones who were given a second chance, but I will never forget the men and women left behind, struggling to be recognized and fighting, to no avail, for a chance at redemption.

I do what I can in other ways as well. Every two months I donate a pint of blood with Upstate New York Transplant Services. I had to wait a year before I was able to do this because that is the law for people who have been in prison for a long time. I recall reading an article while in prison that said that for every pint of blood donated, it can save up to three lives. So far I have donated 25 pints of blood and my goal is 40 pints (five gallons). I have also filled out all of the paperwork so that when I die, my body will be donated to science. I have participated in two clinical studies to find a cure for Multiple Sclerosis. It may not mean much to a lot of people, but I am willing to bet that the people who have used my blood didn't really care where it came from as long as it helped keep them alive. My body will also be used by some medical student who just may find the cure for cancer or some other horrible disease.

Chapter 20

I want to thank you for purchasing this book. Not only is this book a culmination of my dream to share my story with the world, but it is an opportunity for me to touch more lives collectively that I can through speaking engagements. And that's what this is all about: saving lives.

My goal is to get this book into the hands of young people struggling with addiction. I hope it will be read by families who have never considered the possibility that their children are at risk. I want churches to hear this message and know that there is more that needs to be done to fight for the least of us. I want this book on college campuses. I want people in prison to read it. People need to hear the truth. They need to understand the reality of their choices. Our society has become so desensitized to violence, to drugs, to prison. Hollywood and the music industry have taken a brutal reality and distorted, perverted it into flashy television shows on A&E and movies where life in prison resembles a college frat house. In reality, the cleanest, best-run, safest prison in America is the worst place you could ever imagine living.

Each of us has a chance to make a positive difference. A difference in our own lives, but more importantly, a difference in the lives of those around us. As difficult as my life has been, there have been people who have been there for me, people who inspired me even though I may never have met them. People whose help, care, and faith taught me that through my commitment to hard work, faith, dedication and a belief in myself, I could accomplish anything. Their words kept me going through the darkest hours of my life, when it would have been easy to give up. I aim and hope to be that inspiration for you or someone you care about. I want to let you know there are options. I want you to believe there is reason to hope and believe in your own life and possibility. I want you to draw inspiration from my life and my struggles and see that if I could overcome the obstacles placed in my path, then you can, too.

It probably goes without saying, but if I could go back and change anything in my life; it would be what happened on the night of April 23, 1974. I never meant to kill anyone. I never meant for things to get out of control and for so many people to suffer for my actions. I grieve for my victims and their families. If I could sit down across from them, I would tell them how incredibly sorry I am for what happened. I would tell them that I don't expect forgiveness, or compassion for what I've done.

Most of all, I would try to show them that I am trying to make something positive out of the pain and misery I caused. I know it won't bring their loved ones back, but I truly believe, I know, that I have saved lives as I have shared my story with people all over the globe. So, although I don't expect it to bring them any comfort, the deaths of my victims, their loved ones were not in vain.

As I have said many times, I believe everything in life happens for a reason. Would my life have been different if I had grown up in a two-parent suburban home living a run-of-the-mill middle class life? I'm sure it would have. But as author Joan

Walsh Anglund once said: *Adversity often activates a strength we did not know we had.* I was a weak child. I came from a weak family. I grew into a weak adult. But the adversity I faced in my life eventually activated a strength that not only did I not know I had, but no one knew I had. A strength that allowed me to overcome, to persevere and to survive more than 37 years of my life locked in a cage without giving up hope.

As you close this book and find a place for it on your shelf or consider sharing it with someone else, ponder these final thoughts. *You* too have an inner-strength beyond what you know. You are powerful. You are capable of change and good things far beyond your wildest imagination. The world is rarely changed by people whom you might expect it to be. It is more often the everyday man who does extraordinary things.

Channel your adversity and conquer your fears. Erase all doubts about your ability to be everything you dream of. Cut off every option and dread of failure and you will leave yourself with only one path, the path to success. My life hasn't been easy and I suspect yours hasn't been either. But as Anthony Robbins says,

The past does not equal the future. If I had allowed my past to equal my future, I would have continued to live a life of hopeless despair and I would have been dead and gone long before now. I almost let that happen, but through the grace of God; I rose from the ashes and was given a second chance.

Maybe you've already experienced your rebirth. Maybe you are still waiting. Or, maybe you haven't hit rock bottom yet. Wherever you are in your world, stop, take stock of your life and take action now to be the person you want to be. I did it, and you can to. You just have to want it bad enough. If you do, if you are willing to work harder than anybody else, if you are willing to get knocked down and get back up, then the possibilities are endless.

Many people will try to take shortcuts, try to beat the system, try to get one up on people and then wonder why they continually come up short. There is no shortcut to making it in this life. None. If you are one of those people, and I meet them every day, if you think the world owes you something, if you think you got a bum deal and there is nothing you can do about it, then somewhere in your future there is an 8 x 12 cell and a life of unspeakable misery waiting for you.

Be strong, believe, and be faithful to yourself. Good luck on your own journey. I hope that our paths cross one day and I have the chance to shake your hand, to hear your story and to both inspire you and be inspired by you. Because in the end, that is what makes life worth living. It took me 40 years to learn that simple-yet-profound lesson; but once I did, I committed to my own personal transformation and, since then, life has never been sweeter. Good luck and Godspeed.

Acknowledgments

A book like this wouldn't be possible without the support of many people. There have been thousands of people who inspired me to become the person I have become: Counselors, teachers, professors, clergy, neighbors, guards, parole officers, students, law enforcement officials, judges, doctors, lawyers, enemies, writers, and people both in and out of prison, family members and many others.

So I thank each and every one of you. Through my struggles, through my triumphs and tribulations, each of you was there for me. I once knew a man who when you asked how he was doing, he would reply, "More blessed than I deserve." As I write these words, that is how I feel about my life. I am truly more blessed than I deserve.

I am blessed with my health, blessed to be surrounded by good people and blessed to have the opportunity to wake up every day and change lives. I have been given an incredible opportunity, a second chance at life. There is not a day that goes by that I don't thank God for the doors he has opened for me, the people he has put in my path and the wisdom and insight he has afforded me to reach others with my words.

Postscript

Gerald (Jerry) Balone passed away on March 13th 2013. All proceeds from books sold after his death will be donated to New York State Office of Victim Services.

www.ingramcontent.com/pod-product-compliance
Lightning Source LLC
Chambersburg PA
CBHW061305110426
42742CB00012BA/2067